Angels and the Supernatural

Donald Peart

Angels and the Supernatural ©2023 Donald Peart

Bible Translation Used: The King James (Public Domain), NKJV, NIV, BSB, NASB, YLT, etc.

All bold text and literal parenthetical phrases in the Scripture references are added by the author for clarity or were added by the translators of a particular edition for clarity. Single quotes and hyphenated quotes are also used in some text to highlight a literal definition of the original texts for compound words. "Letters" used in a scripture reference (i.e., Proverbs 24:13a), references the first part of the scripture verse before a punctuation, Proverbs 24:13b, is the second part of the verse between punctuation, etcetera. The Hebrew word pictures used in this text is by no means the only interpretation and are not intended to compete with accepted definitions of Hebrew words.

Dictionary reference, includes, but is not limited to, Strong's Concordance, BibleWorks Software, and ISA2 Basic Software, BibleHub.com

Title and lettering recommended by my wife Judith Peart
Front cover art by Charity Peart
Back cover art by Jeshua Peart
Cover design by Donald Peart, Jr.

Hard Cover ISBN: 9798376380352
Paperback Cover: 9798376384879

Acknowledgment

I thank our Lord Jesus who through his Spirit of Truth has taught me throughout the years and continues to teach me the words of Truth. I greatly appreciate the patience and support of my lovely wife, Judith, working with me in the ministry, as she has consistently done throughout the years of our service to the Lord Jesus Christ and to His ecclesia.

Thanks also to those who are colaborers with Judith and me, in the gospel of our Lord Jesus Christ, throughout the years at Crown of Glory Ministries. Some of whom took time out of their busy schedules to review the draft copies of this book to mitigate inadvertent errors or omissions. And as my custom is, I like to name some of them, including our children.

Thanks to Donald Peart Jr and his wife Keyanna Peart, Jeshua Peart, Charity Peart, Benjamin Peart, Jesse Peart, Dameon Gibbs and Tiffany Gibbs, Tia Henry, Larry Summerville Jr. and Tumajah Summerville, Jason Owens and Quinnita Owens, Maria Miller, Kimberli Newman, Cheyanne Brown, Tia Henry, Nichole Brown, Stacey Buzemore and Auntae Buzemore, Tracey Turpin, Cynthia Bryant, Robin Dickerson Wil Gibbs, Michael and Diane Sumler, Anticius and Ja'Nee Bartley, Samuel Esser, Armondo and Adine Horsey, Joyce Hart, Natilie Keys, Terence and Joelle Dorsey, George and Anita Johnson.

May the grace of our Lord Jesus Christ continue to be with your spirits; and may you continue to grow in the grace, knowledge and faith of our Lord Jesus Christ. May you also continue to dwell between the arms of the everlasting heavenly Father.

Table of Contents

Angels

The Lord Jesus has myriads of angels who serve him. He has also delegated angels to minister to those who are heirs of salvation. It follows that angels have always been an interesting topic to humanity. So much so that people often make pictures, statues, paintings, art, some godly, some ungodly, of their understanding of angels.

I remember around 1991 me and Chris, a brother in the Lord Jesus I was mentoring at the time, stayed up all night studying the Book of Job and other books of the Bible seeking understanding concerning angels. At the time, I also read a book or two concerning angels and came away dissatisfied. In fact, I gave up pursuing understanding of angels offered by others; because their teachings seem incomplete; or their teaching on angels appears to deal more with practices God forbids.

However, I did continue to pursue the study of God's Word of Truth, and in the process, the Spirit of Jesus has opened to me an understanding concerning angels. This book is set forth to give a biblically based understanding concerning angels, both the elect and holy angels, other angels, and Satan and his angels. I also briefly discuss how some of the "angels" and "stars" the Lord Jesus defined in the Book of Revelation relate to spirit angels and his human angels.

Thus, this author's intent is to speak of "angels" who are "spirits," and other angels as revealed in the scriptures. The "other angels" to be discussed are various categories of angels and their various functions or workings, whether bad, good or disciplinary.

Malakim — Angels

The Hebrew word for angel is "malak" (מַלְאָךְ). "Malak" is defined as one who is "dispatched as a deputy" (see Strong's Concordance). "Deputy" can be defined as a person who has the immediate right to exercise the same authority as their superior, delegated authority, etcetera. Therefore, angels are God's delegates authorized to execute God's directive as his representative in specific assignments. The strength of this understanding that God deputized angels to serve God and man is seen in Genesis chapter two, where a derivative ["melakah" (מְלָאכָה)] of the Hebrew word for angels ["malak" (מַלְאָךְ).] is used related to God's "work." "Melakah," by understanding the use of the letter "hey" (ה) at the end of a word, means "that which comes from." Thus, God's "work" that is "deputized" to serve his creation, including but is not limited to serving mankind is also executed by angels.

*Genesis 2:1-3, NASB: ¹Thus the heavens and the earth were completed, and all their hosts. ²By the seventh day God completed His **work ("melakah")** which He had done, and He rested on the seventh day from all His **work ("melakah")** which He had done. ³Then God blessed the seventh day and sanctified it, because in it He rested from all His **work ("melakah")** which God had created and made.*

"In the seventh day, God completed his work" to also include but is not limited to the work of the angels deputized to serve God and God's humanity. "In the seventh day, he rested from all his work" with an understanding that God rested from his work; however, the work of the deputized angels continued to work on behalf of God and humanity. "In this seventh day" are God's "blessing" and "sanctification" related to God "rest" from all of his "work" now deputized to humanity and angels.

In other words, in God's creation of the heavens and the earth, God also created angels and deputized them to serve both the

Godhead and humanity. Saying it another way, from the beginning, in God's creation, all of our needs are to be automatically ministered to through the pre-deputized work of God on behalf of humanity. As the writer of Hebrew says, all angels are ministering spirits sent forth to minister through those who are heirs of salvation (Hebrews 1:13-14). The whole creation, the heavens, the earth, and the angels are deputized by God to also take care of his beloved creation, mankind.

Therefore, entering into God rest also includes entering into the knowing that God delegated all of creation to cater to mankind and therefore we are not to be anxious about anything, as Jesus admonished us to walk. The Sabbath was made for man and not man for the Sabbath" (Mark 2:27). According to the Hebrew reading of a portion of Psalm chapter one hundred thirty-nine, verse sixteen, "… days were fashioned for me …." Finally, Jesus taught that the days God fashioned for mankind "cares" automatically to provide for humanity, as God automatically cares for lilies and birds (Matthew 6:25-34).

Angelōi — Angels

The Greek word for angel is "angelos;" and it is literally defined as to bring (or lead) a message. Thus, according to the New Testament Greek definition, angels bring messages from the living God to humanity. They are God's messenger with news, good or bad. In the New Testament God clarified that there are angels called spirits, angels of the Lord or angels of God, the elect angels, the holy angels. There are also angels **not** "standing" in God's "Truth" called Satan and his angels. However, God owns all angels and determines their status with regards to his standard of measure.

Names of Angels

*Genesis 32:29: And Jacob asked him, and said, **tell me**, I pray you, your name.*

*Judges 13:17a: And Manoah said unto **the angel** of the LORD, what is your name ...?*

Through the ages some have been pursuing ascertaining the name of angels; especially "their angels." It appears though that the heavenly Father has elected to only reveal the names of some angels through his prophetic Word of Truth. In the Scriptures of Truth, the Lord Jesus, who created everything, has revealed to us some names of angels that range from Michael, "the great" archangel to some of the "angels that sinned," other angel like Abaddon, the king angel of the abyss, the great star angel Apsinthos, and so on.

I will first begin with the names of some of the holy and elect angels I have found in the Bible, so far: Michael, Gabriel, Palmoni, Palai, and arguably Peniel. I will then follow with biblical understanding with regards to some of the other angels and their functions as it may relate to mankind, some of whom are also named in the Bible. With that said, this book concerning angels is by no means exhaustive with regards to the angels of the Lord.

Michael, the Great Archangel

*Jude 1:9: Yet **Michael the archangel,** when contending with the devil he disputed about the body of Moses, dare not bring against him '**blasphemy**,' but said, the Lord rebuke you.*

In the Book of Jude, Michael is called an archangel. The word "archangel" is transliterated from the Greek compound "arxággelos," from "árxōn," "of the first order, chief" "take precedence," "rule," "to be first," "to begin," "prince" and "ággelos," "angel," "messenger," "delegate." Hence, Michael is a "chief-angel;" he is a "ruler- angel;" he is a "beginning-angel," and so on. In Daniel chapter ten, verse thirteen, Michael is called "one of the chief princes," which can be translated as "one of the head princes." Thus, Michael is a "head" of other angels; and there are other "head" angels or "ruler" angels beside him. Some of these "head" angels are holy and elect; other head angels are of the "angels that sinned;" they "stood not in Truth." In the Book of Revelation that is filled with angels of different orders, and in the Book of Daniel, we learn that Michael has angels that belong to him or angels he rules over as "one of the chief princes." "**Michael and his** angels fought against the dragon" (Revelation 12:7b). "Michael, **one of the chief princes**, came to help me"(Daniel 10:13b). In addition, "archangel" since "arch" can also be translated as beginning, Michael is on of "beginning-angel." Jesus created Michael at the beginning; and Michael is one of the beginnings angels, as a head angel, with other angels under him!

Michael, a Beginning Angel

One of the understandings of Michael being a "beginning" angel is that Jesus created Michael, along with other "deputized angels," in the beginning when Jesus fashioned both the heaven and the earth in the same duration of six days (Genesis 1:1, Exodus 20:11, Genesis 2:1-2). It is also true that

5

Michael is one of the beginning angels who remained "holy" and thus, "elected" with the other "elect angels." And it is also true that some of the beginning angels, like "the prince of this world," Satan, did not remain in the truth. That is, the "principalities," or literally "beginnings" who are currently contending **against** God's people (believing Jews and believing Gentiles) are some of the "beginnings" who became a part of "Satan and his angels;" as opposed to Michael, the **great prince**, an archangel, and other archangels and angels who remained holy to our Lord Jesus Christ and continue to stand up for God's Truth and God's people.

Michael the Great Prince

*Daniel 12:1: And at that time shall **Michael** stand up, **the great prince** which stands for the 'sons' of your people.*

In Daniel chapter twelve, verse one, Michael is called the "great prince." Yes, Michael is one of Jesus' great angels who stands up for God's people. Note, it took **Michael "the great prince"** angel to cast out of heaven "the original serpent, **the great dragon**; and this original serpent was also bound with a **"great chain"** by an angel from heaven (Daniel 12:1, Revelation 12:7-9, Revelation 20:1). Michael, the archangel, had such respect among the other holy angels he is considered "great" in the opinion of the angel Gabriel who called Michael great when Gabriel was speaking to the Prophet Daniel.

And per the angel Gabriel, this great Michael "stands up" for the sons of Daniel's people, which includes but is not limited to the corporate son, the Body of Christ (or God's many sons) made up of believing Jews and believing Ethnics (Ephesians 2:11-19, Revelation 12, Galatians 4:1-7, Romans 8:14-17, etcetera). With that said, it appears that Michael, the archangel, is also seen in other places in the scriptures, in an implicit manner..

Michael Having God's Name

Exodus 23:20-21: *²⁰Behold, I send **an Angel** before you, to keep you in the way, and to bring you into the place which I have prepared. ²¹Beware of him, and obey his voice, provoke him not; for he will not pardon your transgressions: for **my name is in him.***

In the context of these scriptures, the Lord stated that the angel who would lead the Israelites to the promised land was an angel who had **"[God's] name ... in him."** Remember, in light of Daniel chapter twelve, verse one, "**Michael** is ... the great prince who stands for the 'sons' of [Daniel's] people?" In other words, Michael was probably the angel who stood up for Israel, against the enemies of God's sons; when they traveled from Egypt to the promised land and the Lord **authorized the angel with his name** to lead them into the promised land.

There are two to three angels named in the Bible that have the name "God" ("El") in their names. There is Michael, Gabriel and arguably Peniel. (We will discuss the latter two angels later in this book and only focus on Michael here). **"Michael"** is literally translated as **"Who-as-God,"** seen in the parsing of the Hebrew word transliterated as "Michael;" [(מִיכָאֵל), reading from left to right, "Mi"-"מִ"(who) — Kaph-"כָ"(as) — "El"-"אֵל" (God)]. So, in addition to Michael having God's name, **"El,"** in his name, Michael is also "as God" and "like-God." That is, God's name (nature and character) is in Michael, the great prince who stands up for "sons." Thus, one can see that the angel who leads the sons of Israel of whom it is said "[God's] name is in him, " is probably Michael, the archangel.

This truth can be understood from another vantage point. We learned in Daniel chapter twelve, verse one that Michael, "the great prince ... stands up for the sons of [Daniel's] people." Daniel's people at the time of the vision are the Israelites.

However, if one includes the New Testament believing Jews and believing Gentiles, as one Body, as "the Israel of God," as Apostle Paul puts it, the sons of Daniel's people includes the New Testament sons of God (Ephesians 2, Ephesians 3, Romans 11, Galatians 6:16, and so on). In addition, as "Michael, one of the head princes," stands up for the sons of Daniel's people, as an angel that rules in the invisible on their behalf, the Book of Daniel also makes it clear that there are other "prince" angels or "king" angels that rule over nations, then and also now. These angels who are over nations **not** under God's rule do **not stand in the Truth** of the writings of God, the heavenly Father.

Michael, Stand for God's People

For example, "Miachael, the great prince" stands up for natural Israel and the Church, "the Israel of God" through Jesus, the Christ. There is also a "prince" angel that rules over Persia, modern day Iran (Daniel 10:13). There is a "spirit of the kings of the Medes" (Jeremiah 51:11). There is a spirit of the philistines nation, a spirit of the Arabian nation and a spirit of the Ethiopian nation (2 Chronicle 21:16). There is a cherub, who sinned, associated with the kingdom of Tyrus (Ezekiel 28:12-19). There is the dragon Rahab (lit., Storm) associated with Egypt (Isaiah 19:3; 30:1-7; 51:9-10).

It is worthy to note that both the sea and the dragon associated with the sea have a "watcher" angel over them (Job 7:12, comparer Daniel 4). One must ask the question, why do they need to be watched? There is an invisible "prince of Greece" associated with the Greeks (Daniel 10:20). There is a spirit that rules Babylon (Daniel 11:1). Thus, there are satanic ruling principalities in the heavenly places that rule over other nations, small or large, that are not subjected to the "truth" of the living God. It follows that Michael is the great prince who stands up for God's people, the Jews and the Gentiles who believe that Jesus is the Christ, the Son of the living God (Daniel 12:1, Joshua 3, Jude 1:9, Ephesians 2:11-18; 3:1-4, etcetera). In other words, the scriptures make it clear that there are spirits or angels who rule over nations; except the "sons" of the people of God have Michael, the great prince, who stands up for us.

This is clearly seen in the scriptures.[1] If this concept that there are other princes, (again, those angels not standing in the Truth) ruling over nations who do not serve the living God, one can now see one of the reasons why the Lord God sent an angel before the Israelites to bring them into the promised land? That is, invisible princes ruling over nations must be conquered mirrored by conquests related to the kings and princes in the natural. Saying it another way, any heathenistic person who convert to having "faith towards God" in any nation is also related to parallel victories of our angels conquering satanic "beginning" in the invisible (Ephesians 3, Ephesians 6).

When any battle is won in the invisible, related to us acquiring somethings in the Lord through faith in the living God, it will also manifest in the natural. Saying it another way, natural wars on earth are an indication that there are spiritual wars in the heavens; holy and elected princes and their angels, battling other princes of darkness and their angels to bring to pass the writings of Truth (Daniel 10, Revelation 12). For example, the elect angels battle satanic angels to establish God's predetermined time of rule related to God's Truth. This is exemplified in Daniel chapter ten. The time of the prince of Persia's rule came to an end; however, the prince of Persia did not want to relinquish his rule. Thus, Michael came to help Gabriel defeat the prince of Persia, as Gabriel previously helped Michael defeat the spirit of Babylon, when the Babylonian rule had come to an end (Daniel 10:13 through

---

[1] Daniel 10:1 through Daniel 11:1; Daniel 12:1, Revelation 12:1-12, Exodus 23:23, Joshua 5:13-15, Jude 1:9

Daniel 11:1). All of these spiritual activities (wars) in the heavens were mirrored by wars in the natural realm. When Babylon's rule was to end, there was also a natural war in which Cyrus, the Mede, won the war. When Persia's rule was to end, there was a natural war on earth in which Alexander the Great defeated the Persian army and so forth. Thus, when the sons of Israel were to possess Canaan, the angel with God's name was sent with them, so that the spirits that ruled Canaan would be defeated and Joshua and the army of Israel would simultaneously win the war in the natural. Now, I hope the following verses now give a greater understanding.

Exodus: 23;20-23: *²⁰Behold, I send an **Angel before you**, to keep you in the way, and to bring you into the place which I have prepared. ²¹Beware of him, and obey his voice, provoke him not; for he will not pardon your transgressions: **for my name is in him.** ²²But if you shall indeed obey his voice and do all that I speak; then I will be an enemy unto your enemies, and an adversary unto your adversaries. ²³For **my Angel** shall go before you and bring you in unto the Amorites (or publicity), and the Hittites (or terror), and the Perizzites (or lit., separated, open country), and the Canaanites (or humiliation), and the Hivites (or life-giving towns), and the Jebusites (or trampled): and **I will cut them off.***

The "Archsoldier" of God's Power

Here is a question, how did God "cut them off," that is cutting off the occupiers of the promised land? God cut them off both in the invisible by the hand of the "prince" angel, whom I believe is Michael, the great prince, or some other "archsoldier." And in the natural, God cut off the people of the land who did not believe in the Truth of the living God, by the hand of Joshua and the army of Israel. That is, as Joshua was about to invade Jericoh, a "prince" angel appeared to him, and the prince was on either side (he was not against any "believer" in the living God [Jew or Gentiles (i.e., Rahab, the harlot, and her household)].

Joshua 5:13-15: [13]*And it came to pass, when Joshua was by Jericho, that he lifted up his eyes and looked, and behold, there stood a* **man** *over against him with his sword drawn in his hand: and Joshua went unto him, and said unto him, are you for us, or for our adversaries?* [14]*And he said, nay; but as* **'prince'** *of the host of the LORD am I now come. And Joshua fell on his face to the earth, and did worship, and said unto him, what says my lord unto his servant?* [15]*And the* **'prince'** *of the LORD'S host said unto Joshua, Loose your shoe from off your foot; for the place whereon you stand is holy. And Joshua did so.*

This "prince" was an angel from the Lord, in fact, the Septuagint (LXX) Greek translation called this angel an "archsoldier" or "archstrategist" of the power of (the) Lord." According to the Greek Septuagint translation of Joshua chapter five, verse fourteen, the "prince" said to Joshua: "ho de eipen auto ego **archistrategos dynames kyriou;**" translated as "but he said to him, I am **archsoldier** (of the) power (of the) Lord." This then also tells us that there were invisible battles being waged on behalf of the sons of Israel, and a **"archstrategist,"** a **"prince,"** and hence an **arch-warrior,** was directly involved in the battle. Finally, as more proof that Michael, the archangel, stood up for the sons of Daniel's people, it was Michael who contended with the Devil over the body of Moses after Moses died.

Michael and the Body of Moses

Moses,' at age one hundred and twenty, the "natural forces" in his body did not "abate" and his "eye was not dim." Without getting into all the details, the angel named Death did not reign in the body of Moses (Romans 5:14). That is, Moses was one of the seven[2] people (six men and one woman) found in the Bible whom I define as conquering death in their

---

[2] The seven people who conquered Death are: Jesus, Enoch, Melchizedek, Sarah, the daughter of Asher, Moses, Phinehas, and Elijah.

bodies. Thus, God had to command Moses to die, because Death did not reign in Moses' body; and Moses died after God commanded him to die (Deuteronomy 32:49-50). Thus, the Devil then contended over the body of Moses. Why? Would the Devil have used it to institute idol worship as the Devil instituted idol worship with the "brass serpent"[3] God originally told Moses to use it as a means to heal the Israelites from serpents bites?

It took Michael, the archangel, to rebuke the Devil in the name of the Lord (Jesus) to secure the body of Moses' unto the Lord; and "no man knows of his sepulcher unto this day" (Deuteronomy 34:6). In fact, the last record of Moses is that he appeared "in glory," resurrection form, to the Lord Jesus in the holy mountain. This occurred when our Lord Jesus manifested "his coming in power" in transmigration.

*Jude 1:9: Yet **Michael the archangel,** when contending with the Devil he disputed about **the body of Moses,** dare not bring against him **'blasphemy,'** but said, the Lord rebuke you.*

*Luke 9:28-30: ²⁸And it came to pass about an eight days after these sayings, [Jesus] took Peter and John and James, and went up into a mountain to pray. ²⁹And as he prayed, the fashion of his countenance was altered, and his raiment was white and glistering. ³⁰And, behold, there talked with him two men, which were **Moses** and Elias: ³¹Who appeared **in glory,** and spoke of his **'exodus'** which he should accomplish at Jerusalem.*

Moses and Elijah were the two men who spoke with Jesus concerning Jesus' "exodus" from the earth back into the heavens, which was to transpire through his death, burial, resurrection, and ascension. These two men appeared to Jesus "in glory," in their glorified bodies. Elijah appearing "in glory" is easier for some to understand; because Elijah was translated and thus glorified without experiencing death.

---

[3] Numbers 21:9, 2 Kings 18:4

Moses, though, even though he conquered Death, death had no dominion over Moses through his unique relationship with the Lord, eventually experienced death at the command of the Lord God. However, sometime after Moses' death, the Devil attempted to contend for Moses' body; and Michael rebuked him for it. The Lord eventually resurrected Moses as seen in the fact that Moses also appeared "in glory" (resurrected form) to our Lord Jesus. Therefore, both men could tell the Lord Jesus of their experiences relative to ascension, death, burial, and eventual resurrection.

Moses could tell Jesus of his experience relative to death and eventual resurrection; and Elijah could tell Jesus of his experience of ascension without dying. And with regards to the truth that Michael, the archangel, was intensely involved with the sons of Israel in their traveling to the promised land and in their inheriting the promised land, Jude named the "angel ... with God's name in him" as "Michael, the archangel" who was present among the people of God to contend with the Devil over Moses' body after Moses died.

"**Michael**, (is) **the great prince** who stands for the 'sons' of your people" (Daniel 12:1). It was/is Michael and his angels who fought and displaced the great dragon and his angels out of heaven after the woman produced God's corporate male, son (Revelation 12). Thus, Michael stands in the Truth on behalf of the sons of natural Israel, and for the sons of spiritual Israel (the Israel of God) through our Lord Jesus Christ.

Gabriel, an Archangel

*Luke 1:19: The **angel** answering said unto him, **I am Gabriel,** that stand in the presence of God; and am sent to speak unto you, and to show you these glad tidings.*

*Luke 1:26-27; 30: [26]And in the sixth month **the angel Gabriel** was sent from God unto ... a virgin espoused to a man whose name was Joseph, of the house of David; and the virgin's name was **Mary** ... [30]And the angel said unto her ... behold, you shall conceive in your womb, and bring forth a son, and shalt call his name JESUS.*

*Daniel 9:21: Yes, while I was speaking in prayer, even **the man Gabriel,** whom I had seen in the vision at the beginning, being '**tired, tired'** touched me about the time of the evening oblation.*

*Daniel 8:16: And I heard a man's voice between the banks of Ulai, which called, and said, **Gabriel,** make this man to understand the vision.*

Gabriel is also another prominent angel named in the Bible. Gabriel is one of the four prominent angels named in the Talmud. Gabriel is also named as one of the archangels in Enoch 1, portion of which is quoted in the Book of Jude. It is my understanding that Gabriel is also one of the "prince" angels or "head" angels, making him an archangel. In the Book of Daniel chapter ten, verse thirteen, we learn that Gabriel battled two invisible "kings of Persia" (one was a prince of the Medes, and the other was the "prince of Persia").

It follows that in order for Gabriel to take on "princes" (or "arch" spirits) in the invisible, he is understood to be a "prince," an "archangel," or a chief angel himself. In fact the two kings of Persia, consisting of the ruling spirit of Medes and the ruling "prince" of the Persians, outnumbered Gabriel two to one; and Michael one of the head princes had to come and help Gabriel to balance the conflict; and they eventually defeated and bound both kings of Persia to God's truth, so the way could be made for the spirit of Greece to rule next, according to God's plan noted in the "writings of truth" (Daniel 11:20-21). The holy and elect "prince" angels battle other princes of darkness who stood not in the Truth. God is not going to send an underling angel to battle prince angels. The princes are too strong for the other angels subordinated to prince angels or archangels. For example, the "prince of this world," the great dragon, is directly handled by the "great prince," Michael, "**one** of the chief princes" (Jude 1:9, Revelation 12:7-8).

The same is true for Gabriel as indicated in Daniel chapter ten, verse thirteen, Daniel chapter ten, verse twenty-one and Daniel chapter eleven, verse one, Gabriel along with Michael directly fights other princes, like the prince of Babylon, the kings of Persia, to enforce God's duration of rule according to the writing of Truth; and for Gabriel to bring to us (God's people in the earth) "truth" written in the "scripture of truth," that is enforced by all of God's holy and elect angels. Hence, Gabriel is understood to be an archangel, God's mighty-man!

Gabriel is transliterated from the Hebrew word גַּבְרִיאֵל reading from left to right. "Giber" (גֶּבֶר) means mighty-man, powerful-man, warrior, strong-man. The Hebrew letter "yad" (י) just after "Giber" means "my;" and then "El" (אֵל) means "God." Therefore, the angel Gabriel is "God's, [seen in "yad" ("my")] mighty-man," "God's warrior," "God's powerful-man." More importantly, the angel Gabriel is also one of the angels who announces times and events related to our Lord Jesus.

In Luke chapter one, Gabriel announces Jesus' conception of the Holy Spirit and Jesus' name. In Daniel chapter nine, it was Gabriel who explained to Daniel what the seventy weeks meant relative to the coming of the Messiah, the coming of our Lord Jesus in the flesh, and his eventual crucifixion that ended animal sacrifices forever. Also, in Luke chapter one, it was Gabriel that announced the conception of John, the

Baptist, and gave instruction of how John is to live and gave understanding of how John is to introduce the Messiah, the Lord Jesus. Thus, it can be concluded that the archangel Gabriel gives "understanding" concerning the prophetic things related to Jesus, the Son of the living God. Gabriel gives knowledge of what is written in the scriptures of truth. It was also Gabriel that gave us, exemplified through the prophet Daniel, Gabriel also gave us a glimpse of the invisible spiritual activities among the "prince" angels.

Gabriel, Giver of Understanding

Daniel 8:15-17, NASB: *[15]When I, Daniel, had seen the vision, I sought to understand it; and behold, standing before me was one who looked like a man. [16]And I heard the voice of a man between the banks of Ulai, and he called out and said, "**Gabriel, give this man an understanding** of the vision." [17]So he came near to where I was standing, and when he came I was frightened and fell on my face; but he said to me, "**Son of man, understand** that the vision pertains to the time of the end."*

The archangel Gabriel communed with the beloved Prophet Daniel at various times as documented in the Book of Daniel. Gabriel is first introduced by name to Daniel in Daniel chapter eight. In Daniel chapter eight, Daniel saw in a vision the coming war between the Greeks and the confederacy of Medes and the Persians, understood by the two horns on the ram and the goat with one great horn that defeated the ram. In the vision, Gabriel was directed to give Daniel understanding of the vision. However, the writing of in Daniel chapter eight, verse sixteen and seventeen, for the word "understanding" provided great insight into "understanding" that comes from Jesus, the Son of God and understanding that also relates to the sons of God. The phrase "Gabriel, give this man an **understanding** of the vision" can be written as "Gabriel, 'the-son this (man)' of the vision." Before I develop this verse, the same convention of the writing for the word "understanding" as "the-son" is used in Daniel chapter eight, verse seventeen. The Phrase "Son of man, **understand** that the vision pertains to the time of the end" can also be translated as "**the-son**, son of man that to the time of the end the vision." Thus, "understanding" is related to the "Son," Jesus the Christ. Allow me to explain. Jesus said to the Jews "You search the scriptures because you think that in them you have eternal life; **it is these that testify about Me**" (John 5:39). The Greek word translated as "about" is "peri" and it means all about and all about. This means, the "scriptures" are "all about" Jesus.

It follows that the inflection of the word translated as "understanding" is literally translated as "the-son," ["haben" (הבן)]. Thus, all spiritual understanding and revelation knowledge comes from the Spirit of the Son of God (Ephesians 1:17, Luke 10:22, Galatians 1:15-16, 2 Corinthians 2). This means that even in the vision that Daniel saw with respect to the coming war between the Medes and the Persians against the Greeks (Alexander the great and his army), Jesus is a central theme.

Gabriel is then the revealer of the "understanding" that "the-son," is related to Jesus, "the-Son" of God. That is, when the vision is being fulfilled "in the latter times," or "in hind parts time," a fierce king, one of the four kings of Alexander divided kingdom arising after his death, will exalt himself against the "Prince of prince," Jesus (Revelation 1:15). However, Jesus, "the Prince of the kings of the earth" will break this arrogant king without hands! Thus, Gabriel gave "the understanding" that "the-Son," Jesus will prevail against any and all kings of the earth and their kingdoms in the "hind parts" days.

Gabriel, Binder of Princes

Daniel 10:21-11:1-2a, NASB: [21]*"However, I will tell you what is inscribed in* **the writing of truth**. *Yet there is no one who* **stands firmly** *with me against these forces except* **Michael your prince**. [11:1]*"In the first year of Darius the Mede,* **I arose to be an encouragement** *and* **a protection** *for him.* [11:2a]*"And now I will tell you the* **truth** ....*

In Daniel chapter ten, we learn that the archangel Gabriel encountered difficulty reaching Daniel for approximately twenty-one (21) days with regards to Daniel prayer. In Daniel, chapter ten, Gabriel also revealed to Daniel that the holdup was due to the spirit kings of Persia (the invisible princes of Medes and Persians kingdom). However, as we have discussed in this book, the archangel Michael came to Gabriel's aid. After Michael and Gabriel restrained the kings of Persians (consisting of both the spirit of the Medes and the spirit of Persia) allowing Gabriel to reach Daniel, Gabriel began to give Daniel more insight into the invisible. Gabriel revealed to Daniel that there is "writing of truth," and this writing of truth is intended to be revealed to God's people on the earth and enforced with other princes who do not stand in the Truth.

In addition, Gabriel also revealed that Michael, the prince angel who stands up for the people of Daniel was the only one who stood firmly with Gabriel in the writing of Truth which relates to the Persians and the Greeks. Gabriel also goes on to say that He stood with Michael when the rule of the spirit king of Babylon was over, and the writings of Truth dictated that it was time to establish the Medes and Persian empire for a season. With all the context given above, I will now explain further. God's plans are "written in the writings of Truth," or as some translate it, "the Book of Truth."

In this Book of Truth, it is stated that all the four earthly kingdoms God revealed to king Nebuchadnezzar in a dream as four beautiful metals, and God revealed to the Prophet Daniel in a vision as four beasts, all have a duration for their respective world order (Daniel 2, Daniel 7, Daniel 8, Daniel 10-Daniel 12). In addition, all four of these kings and their kingdoms are ruled by an invisible prince angel of the satanic order—those spirits or angels who stood not in the Truth. Thus, when God is ready to terminate the time of each beast's international rule, they tend to fight against the writings of Truth that state their demise and duration of rule. In addition Gabriel reveals that he and Michael, one of the archangels, are the ones who "bind" these princes of darkness to God's allotted time of their world order.

The phrase translated as "stands firmly" in Daniel chapter ten, verse twenty-one is also defined by Strong's Concordance as "to bind" or to "use strength." That is, Michael, in this encounter, was the only other prince angel available to help Gabriel "bind" the prince of Persia to what is written in the Book of Truth. The time of the rule or the time of the world order of the Persians came to an end and the archangels Gabriel and Michael enforced this truth, though the "arch" prince of Persia resisted for a time. What was this prince of Persia resisting? He was resisting the truth that the time of his rule had ended and the time of rule of the spirit of Greece had taken effect.

This truth is also understood with regards to the previous encounter when the invisible king of Babylon was deposed in order for the invisible princes of the Medes and Persia to rule. Gabriels said, in Daniel chapter eleven, verse one: "In the first year of Darius the Mede, I (Gabriel) arose 'to -bind' and 'fortify' for him (Michael)." That is, Darius was the first king of the Medes; and in Daniel chapter five, we learn that the Babylonian kingdom was defeated making way for the kings of Medes and Persians, the rule beginning with Darius. However, the same way as the kings of the Persians resisted Gabriel, when the Greek's rule was to take effect, the invisible spirit of Babylon resisted Michael binding him, and thus, Gabriel came to fortify Michael and to aid Michael in binding the prince of Babylon. That is, the truth of the Persians rule being established was enforced by both Michael and Gabriel.

This same principle of archangels like Gabriel and Michael enforcing the duration of any particular nation or kingdom's rule is true today. In the year 2022, we are in the beginning of the end of the world order as we know it being changed. And like it was in the days of king Nebuchadnezzar, the days of king Darius, and the days of king Alexander, there were wars in the earth mirroring the resistance warring in the invisible against the writing of Truth. However, as it was then, so it is now, warring will continue until the current ruling spirits of this world order are bound for the next spirits to rule come — the great dragon, the beast from the abyss and the false prophet from the earth. With regards to "the beast," the leopard beast, with a lion's mouth and feet like a bear, this "leopard" represents the "spirit of Greece"[4] that will rule the world and control the behavior of humanity to pervert some.

With that said, in 1992, while on a fast, on the ninth (9th) day of the fast, it was my first fast going beyond 3 days. My body was without strength; and as I rested on the sofa while my beloved Judith fixed me some soup; I came to be in a trance and heard a voice say, "The way is being made for the spirit of Greece." I then heard a voice say, "A great tragedy shall happen in America," as I heard the voice speak, I saw president Bush standing upon a pile of rubble exactly as President Bush did after "9/11," eleven years earlier in 1992. I then heard the voice say, "After the tragedy, I will bring forth the Boy Scouts. "The way is being made for the spirit of

---

[4] To get an understanding of the spirit of Greece, I recommend studying the ancient Greek culture, especially in the days of Alexander the Great since the leopard beast with its four wings of a fowl in Daniel 7 represents that time period (see also Daniel 8).

Greece," also called the invisible "prince of Greece," also called the leopard beast in Daniel chapter seven and Revelation thirteen.

Finally, when God's allotted time for the last satanic world order rule to end, the same is to happen to the original serpent, the great dragon. Satan, the great dragon, will be bound with a great chain, imprisoned in the abyss, being bound as the scripture of Truth is enforced. Per Revelation chapter twenty, verses one through six, it is commonly taught and understood that at the end of approximately six thousand years from the first Adam, God will bind the original serpent, God will perform the first resurrection of all his saints; and his saints are to rule the earth "with Christ" as kings and priests unto God for one thousand years.

In Revelation chapter twenty, verses one through three, after the three and a half years rule of "the beast," Satan is "bound" by an angel with a "great chain." It is said that Satan will be bound for a thousand years. This is similar to what Gabriel and Michael did to the satanic princes of Babylon, Medes, Persians, and the Greeks when the Romans took over, and so on. Yes, God's elect and holy angels bind princes of darkness to an allotted time to make sure the writings of Truth are fulfilled.

*Revelation 20:1-3, NASB: ¹Then I saw an angel coming down from heaven, holding the key of the abyss and a great chain in his hand. ²And he laid hold of the dragon, the **serpent of old,** who is the devil and Satan, and **bound him for a thousand years;** ³and he threw him into the abyss, and shut it and sealed it over him, so that he would not deceive the nations any longer, until the thousand years were completed; after these things he must be released for a short time.*

Gabriel and the Scripture of Truth

Daniel 10:21, NASB: ²¹*"However, I will tell you what is inscribed in **the writing of truth**. Yet there is no one who **stands firmly** with me against these forces except **Michael your prince.***

Our Lord Jesus was very meticulous about fulfilling the scriptures or emphasizing that the scriptures must be fulfilled; and therefore, the holy and elect angels do the same as Gabriel indicated. Before I develop the "writing of Truth" or the "Scripture of Truth" relative to Gabriel, here is an example of Jesus stating that the "scriptures" must be fulfilled. This occurred when they were about to unjustly arrest Jesus with weapons, and the apostle Peter stood up in an attempt to defend Jesus. Yet, Jesus tempered their help and told his disciples of his right as an heir of God to request twelve legions of angels to defend him. However, to this point, Jesus did not exercise this right that scriptures may be fulfilled. Jesus had to be crucified at the hands of sinners as prewritten in the "Book of Truth."

Matthew 26: 51-54, NASB: ⁵¹*And behold, one of those who were with Jesus reached and **drew out his sword and struck the slave of the high priest and cut off his ear.** ⁵²Then Jesus said to him, "Put your sword back into its place; for all those who take up the sword shall perish by the sword. ⁵³"Or do you think that I cannot appeal to My Father, and He will at once put at My disposal more than twelve legions of angels? 54"**How then will the Scriptures be fulfilled,** which say that it must happen this way?"*

With that said, Gabriel, Michael also enforces obedience to the writing of truth in the invisible. They make sure "what" is written is "what" happens just as Jesus said if he resisted the unjust arrest, **"how then will the scriptures be fulfilled, which say it must happen this way?"** It follows that it was initially Gabriel and then an unnamed angel of the Lord whom the Lord God sent to Mary and Joseph to reveal the

Truth of Jesus' virgin birth that the scripture which was spoken by the Lord might be fulfilled.

Matthew 1:26-32, NASB: ²⁶*Now in the sixth month the **angel Gabriel** was sent from God to a city in Galilee called Nazareth, ²⁷to a **virgin** engaged to a man whose name was **Joseph,** of the descendants of David; and the virgin's name was **Mary.** ²⁸And coming in, he said to her, "Greetings, favored one! The Lord is with you." ²⁹But she was very perplexed at this statement and kept pondering what kind of salutation this was. ³⁰The angel said to her, "Do not be afraid, Mary; for you have found favor with God. ³¹"**And behold, you will conceive in your womb and bear a son, and you shall name Him Jesus.** ³²"He will be great and will be called the Son of the Most High; and the Lord God will give Him the throne of His father David.*

Matthew 1:18-23: ¹⁸*Now **the birth of Jesus Christ** was as follows: when His mother Mary had been betrothed to Joseph, before they came together she was found to be with child by the Holy Spirit. ¹⁹And Joseph her husband, being a righteous man and not wanting to disgrace her, planned to send her away secretly. ²⁰But when he had considered this, behold, **an angel of the Lord** appeared to him in a dream, saying, "Joseph, son of David, do not be afraid to take Mary as your wife; for the Child who has been conceived in her is of the Holy Spirit. ²¹"She will bear a Son; and you shall call His name Jesus, for He will save His people from their sins." ²²Now all this took place **to fulfill what was spoken by the Lord through the prophet:** ²³"BEHOLD, THE VIRGIN SHALL BE WITH CHILD AND SHALL BEAR A SON, AND THEY SHALL CALL HIS NAME IMMANUEL," which translated means, "GOD WITH US."*

The writing above makes it clear that Jesus had to be of virgin birth **"to fulfill what was spoken by the Lord through the prophet."** And not only did the Lord speak about what was to happen, Isaiah also wrote the scripture that it is to happen, and it did happen as God said it would. Jesus was born of the virgin Mary. So, just as the Lord Jesus does what is necessary to ensure the fulfillment of the scripture while he walked on earth in the flesh, Gabriel also uses "strength" to bind the other angels who stand not in the writing of Truth. As Gabriel said, "I will show you that which is noted in **the scripture of truth:** and there is none that **holds (or binds, or use strength)** with me in these things, but Michael your prince" Why is this important to know?

Satan(s) would love to have God's Word not be fulfilled in its time so they can continue to accuse the Lord and his people. However, Jesus said "scripture cannot be broken" when Jesus confirmed his "equality with God" in John chapter ten, verse thirty-five. "There is no wisdom or understanding or counsel against the Lord" (Proverbs 21:30). Not one angel, not one human, not one creature, not one created thing can alter the Truth of God. Whatever God writes as the "Truth" will be fulfilled; and Gabriel and Michael enforces the Truth of God that is to be fulfilled in its time!

*Daniel 10:21, NASB "However, I will tell you what is inscribed in the **writing of truth**. Yet there is no one who stands firmly with me [Gabriel] against these forces except **Michael** your prince."*

*2 Timothy 2:15: Study to show yourself approved unto God, a workman that needs not to be ashamed, rightly dividing **the word of truth.***

John 8:44: You are of your father the Devil, and the lusts of your father you will do. He was a murderer from the beginning, and **abode (lit., stood) not in the truth, because (Greek, "hoti," as a conjunction, demonstrative, "that"[5]) there is no truth in**

---

[5] "That," the demonstrative result, there is no truth in the Devil is because he did not stand in the Truth. In other words, the Devil had the opportunity to stand in the Truth, however, Jesus said, the "Devil ... stood not in the Truth." This same principle is spoken of the spirit of Antichrist and the Devil in 1 John 2 through 1 John 4.

him. When he speaks a lie, he speaks of his own: for he is a liar, and the father of it.

*Ephesians 1:13: In whom [Christ] you also trusted, after that you heard **the word of truth, the gospel of your salvation:** in whom also after that you believed, you were sealed with that holy Spirit of promise.*

*James 1:18, NKJV: Of His own will **He brought us forth** by the **word of truth,** that we might be a kind of firstfruits of His creatures.*

Palai, an Angel of the Lord

*Judges 13:18: And the **angel of the LORD** said unto him, why ask you thus after my name, **seeing it is secret?***

In the scriptures, it is clear that there are "angels of the Lord" and "angels of God;" just as the Word of God also makes it clear that there are "prophets of the Lord" as opposed to "prophets of the people" or "prophets of Baal." "Palai" or "Pilai" is an angel of the Lord Jesus. "Pilai," or "Palai" is transliterated from the Hebrew word פֶּלִאי; and this angel's name is associated with another name of an angel mentioned in the scriptures, "Palmoni."

"Palai" is used in the scripture reference above when the angel is asked his name by the father to be of Sampson in Judges chapter thirteen, verse seventeen. The phrase as translated in the King James version "why ask you thus after my name, seeing it is secret," is literally translated as "why do you ask this my name, and '**it is Palai**'" That is, as Manoah, Sampson's father to be, asked the angel's name that spoke to him about the coming conception and birth of Sampson, the angle inquired of Manoah asking why did he want to know his name; and in the angels' response, the angel gave his name "**it is Palai.**"

Angel Worship Forbidden

With that said, before I develop a definition of the name of this angel, let me show why he appears to be reluctant to give his name and questioned Manoah as to why he needed to know his name. Manoah and his wife were very eager to prepare a "kid" for the angel because they originally thought he was a natural man of God ((Judges 13:8; 13:16). This angel was well aware of the consequences of worshiping angels because of what the original serpent caused to happen [creature worshiping creature, <u>in lieu</u> of creatures worshiping the Creator, God (Romans 1:22-25)]. Thus, the angel warned them in Judges chapter thirteen, verse sixteen not to worship him. "And the angel of the LORD said unto Manoah, though you detain me, I will not eat of your bread: **and if you will offer a burnt offering, you must offer it unto the LORD.** For Manoah knew not that he was an angel of the LORD." This "angel of the Lord," among many angels of the Lord, made it clear that worshiping of angels is unacceptable; and he was as concerned that they may use his name in angel worship, a forbidden act; or man of God worship also a forbidden act (Colossians 2:18; Revelation 19:10, Acts 10: 25-26, Revelation 22:8-9). Thus, in his apparent reluctance, the angel did eventually reveal his name **"it is Palai."**

Wonderful Worker

Judges 13:18, ISV: The angel of the LORD answered him, "Why are you asking this about my name? **It's 'Wonderful.'"**

"Wonderful" is translated from the Hebrew word 'Pilai" or "Palai." "Palai" is also translated as "miracle" and "secret." "Palai" is translated as "wonderful" in Psalms 139:6 when David spoke of the knowledge that God, personally laid hands on David. With that said, this angel's name is "Wonderful," and he does "wondrously." This is seen when the angel of the Lord demonstrated his name in the fire that ascended with the offering to the Lord Jesus from Manoah's.

In other words, this angel is created by God to do "wonders," miracles and signs as a sign to those whom he is sent with predictive words from the Lord Jesus. Let us look at the wonderful act this angel performed as a sign the Lord sent him to Manoah and his wife, while at the same time this angel was firm in preventing any worshiping of angels or worshiping of created beings (man, beasts, angels, or spirits).

Judges 13:19-21: [19]So Manoah took a kid with a meat offering and offered it upon a rock **unto the LORD: and the angel did** *wondrously; and Manoah and his wife looked on.* ²⁰*For it came to pass, when the flame went up toward heaven from off the altar, that the* **angel of the LORD ascended in the flame of the altar.** *And Manoah and his wife looked on it and fell on their faces to the ground.* ²¹*But the angel of the LORD* **did no more appear to Manoah and to his wife.** *Then Manoah knew that* **he was an angel of the LORD.**

This reference makes it clear that this angle does wonders. He was able to be seen ascending in the flame of the altar as he disappeared from their sight. He also made it a point not to appear to them again. This to me points to the truth that this angel because he is gifted to do wonders, was careful not to instigate any worshiping of himself, an angel. This worshiping of angels will be developed later in the chapter on the "religion of angels."

Palmoni, a Holy Angel

*Daniel 8:13: Then I heard one **saint** speaking, and another **saint** said unto that **certain saint** which spoke, how long shall be the vision concerning the daily sacrifice, and the transgression of desolation, to give both the sanctuary and the host to be trodden under foot?*

Here is how the first portion of the verse above can also be translated from the Hebrew text.

*Daniel 8:13: And I heard one '**holy one**' speaking and said to one '**holy one**' '**Palmoni**' who was speaking, how long shall be the vision ....*

It is clear in this vision the beloved Prophet Daniel saw that there are some invisible "holy ones." These "holy ones" are called Jesus "holy angels" in Matthew chapter twenty-five, verse thirty-one and "watchers" in Daniel chapter four. They remained holy and committed the Lord Jesus when Satan and his angels remained not in the Truth. In the Book of Daniel chapter eight, verse thirty-one, the name of one of these holy angels is revealed as "Palmoni." However, before I develop the name of this holy angel, be mindful that all of the angels of the Lord demonstrate some facet of God nature or power; and some of them are representative or types of our Lord Jesus Christ.

Nature of Angels of the Lord

In Daniel chapter ten, verses one through six, the description of Gabriel, the archangel, is almost similar to the Lord Jesus' description in Revelation chapter one, verses thirteen through sixteen. Gabriel's face is like lightning. Jesus' face is like the power of the sun. Gabriel's eyes were like a lamp of fire. Jesus's eyes were a flame of fire. Gabriels' feet were like polished bronze. Jesus's feet were also like bronze. It follows that Palmoni also demonstrates the character of Jesus Christ, the mystery of Christ.[6] That is, Jesus is the Wonderful One; Jesus is God's secret (the once hidden mystery), hidden from the angels in their plain sight. The mystery of Christ was hidden in God from the angels (principalities and authorities), ages and generations (Ephesians 3:9-11, Colossians 1:26, 1 Corinthians 2:7-8). With that said, the intent of this book is to show the workings of Palmoni, as a holy angel.

Palmowni Defined

Per Strong's Concordance, **"Palmowni"** is from two Hebrew root words. It is derived from an obsolete noun, **paalown,** and/or from the verb **paalaah,** to distinguish, put a difference, show marvelous, separate, set apart, sever, make **wonderfully** (see Strong's Concordance), and is united with the word **"almoni,"** which means one concealed , unknown one, silent one or **secret one.** However, the Hebrew roots can be understood as such, "palah," "wonderful" and "manah" to count, number, recon, weigh, etcetera (see E. W. Bullinger, *Number in the Scripture*).

In the context of Daniel chapter eight, verse twenty-three, one holy one asked Palmoni, who is also a holy one, the duration related to the transgression of desolation. This duration was specifically given by Palmoni, because he understands the "secrets" of "numbers" and he is a "wonderful-numberer" as his name depicts. He sets durations as the living God assigns him to do according to God's will and plans.

Palmowni, Numberer of Secrets

Before I continue, I must give caution here by saying this truth should not be taken as an opportunity to interpret every numeric value we experience in our daily lives as some secret

---

[6] Please reference one of my books, titled, *The Last Hour, the First Hour, the Forty-second Generation*

communication from the living God. God does not want us to seek numbers for directions as some erroneously govern their lives by lottery and other numeric. **It is the Holy Spirit of Jesus who leads and governs us!** Yet in the scripture, God placed secrets concerning our Lord Jesus Christ relative to numbers; and the holy angel, Palmoni is a holy angel related to issuing durations related to numbers and the secrets in these numbers. For example, the number three (3) in the Hebrew texts of the Bible, as revealed through the Spirit of Jesus Christ, shows Jesus as the "nailed-authority" between two "devourers" (the two thieves on the cross). Remember all the "writings" testifies of Jesus (John 5:39). Here is an excerpt from my book, *The Numbers of God;* where the secrets related to Jesus, the Christ, in the number three (3) is explained as such:

Jesus, the Secret in "Three"

"Three is representative of "**Jesus crucified between the thieves, the nailed authority between the two thieves. Jesus' resurrection, threefold principles:** "Have not I written to you **excellent things (lit., threefold things**) in counsels and knowledge" (Proverbs 22:20). Three is the Hebrew word shlush (שלוש). The Hebrew spelling for three (3) sometimes augments the Hebrew letter "vav" (ו) into the other spelling of three (שלש), with "vav" pictured as a nail, tent peg, or to be joined. The Hebrew word picture or pictograph for this spelling of three (3) shlush (שלוש) is the nailed authority between the two devourers or biters, or the nailed shepherd pressed between the two thieves. The nailed (ו) authority (ל) or the nailed(ו) Shepherd's rod (ל) is Jesus symbolized by (לו). The Hebrew letter (ש) means to bite, to press, to devour. Hence, Jesus was crucified (nailed) between the two devouring ones (the evil actors)."

Palmowni, and Nebuchadnezzar

Finally, it appears that Palmoni can also be seen in Daniel chapter four; because Palmowni, the secret numberer, is listed among the "holy ones" in Daniel chapter eight. It follows that in Daniel chapter four, the holy ones, the watchers, were also involved in the numbering of the "seven times" duration of God's humbling of king Nebuchadnezzar. The "secret" related to the "number" "seven times" is also seen in the Hebrew definitions for "times." One of the definitions for "times" speaks of the monthly ministration of a woman. Hence, the "seven times" can speak of a "seven month" period through which God purges Nebuchadnezzar of his unclean attitude against the poor; and his unclean attitude of worshiping the works of his hands; and his unclean attitude of his arrogance against God.

Peniel, God's Angel

Hosea 12:2-4, NKJV: *²The Lord also brings a charge against Judah and will punish **Jacob** according to his ways; according to his deeds He will recompense him. ³He took his brother by the heel in the womb, and in his strength **he struggled with God**. ⁴Yes, he struggled **with the Angel** and prevailed; He wept and sought favor from Him. He found Him in Bethel, And there He spoke to us.*

Genesis 32;24-30: *²⁴And Jacob was left alone; and there **wrestled a man with him** until the breaking of the day. ²⁵And when he saw that he prevailed not against him, he touched the hollow of his thigh; and the hollow of Jacob's thigh was out of joint, as he wrestled with him. ²⁶And he said, Let me go, for the day breaks. And he said, I will not let you go, except you bless me. ²⁷And he said unto him, what is your name? And he said, Jacob. ²⁸And he said, your name shall be called no more Jacob, but Israel: for as a prince hast thou power with God and with men, and hast prevailed. ²⁹**And Jacob asked him, and said, tell me, I pray you, your name.** And he said, 'why' is it that you dost ask after my name? And he blessed him there. ³⁰And Jacob called the name of the place **Peniel:** for I have **seen God face to face**, and my life is preserved.*

In the Old Testament, encounters with angels are usually understood by the recipients as encounters with God, himself. That is, the encounters were indeed with angels; yet the record would also show God speaking in first person to the person who encountered the angel. For example, Moses and the angel in the burning bush, the angel of the Lord is understood to be God, himself, speaking to Moses in Exodus chapter three; however, it is confirmed in Acts chapter seven, verses thirty through thirty-six to be an angel and the Lord in the same encounter. When Manoah, Samson's father and his wife encountered the "angel of God" or "the angel of the Lord," they originally thought he was a "man of God" and later also thought he was "God" (Judges 13:6-6; 16-22). The same is true for Jacob when he encountered an angel, also called a "man," Jacob thought he saw God "face to face" as Sampson's father and mother thought they saw God's face in the angel they experienced.

The Angel Wrestled with Jacob

Jacob's experience with the "man that wrestled with him;" and not Jacob initiating the wrestling, but the man," was actually an angel of God wrestling with Jacob according to Hosea chapter twelve, verse four. This angelic encounter with Jacob occurred at the time of what has come to be known as "the time of Jacob's trouble" (Genesis 35:1-3; Jeremiah 30:7). The "trouble" was related to Jacob's brother Esau whom Jacob tricked out of his birthright; and how he had to face both his brother and his own trickster nature. That is, his imminent facing of his brother placed Jacob into tribulation; and in that time of tribulation; he encountered angels and an angel that I believe to be named "Peniel."

At this encounter, the "man," the "angel" wrestled with Jacob. However, the angel was surprised by the strength of Jacob when Jacob fought back and now had the angel in his grip. This "strength" of Jacob demonstrated in the grasping of the angel, gave us a peek into the strength of the human spirit God gave us which strength will be demonstrated more maturely in the "world to come." In this "world to come" God's "sons of man" will rule during the millennium and not angels (Hebrews 2). The human spirit is stronger than angels and our apparent inferiority is only for a short while until God "brings many sons to glory" (see Hebrews 2).

Acknowledging the Old Nature

With that said, when the tide was turned in the wrestling match in Jacob's favor, and Jacob now refuses to let the angel go, instead of the other way around, the angel asked Jacob to let him go because the day was dawning (Genesis 32:24-26). Jacob responded by saying he would not let the angel go until the angel blessed him. However, because of Jacob's request for a blessing, now the angel also had an upper hand. Jacob had to acknowledge what the wrestling was about in the first place before the angel would bless Jacob. Jacob had to acknowledge his "name" (nature and character) that he was indeed a "trickster," who stole Esau's birthright.

Jacob's trickster nature which started at birth when Jacob took ahold of Esau' heel and later materialized when Jacob disguised himself as Esau and tricked their father to bless him with the blessing of the birthright, instead of Esau, now had to be acknowledged. This admitting of his trickster nature was now "Jacob's trouble;" because Jacob had to meet his full grown brother who had four hundred (400) men coming to meet Jacob and his family. Thus, once the angel had the upper hand by speaking to the "trouble" of Jacob, speaking to his trickster nature, after a night of wrestling, Jacob acknowledged his name and nature, "and [the angel] said what is your name?" And he said Jacob" (Genesis 32:27).

Jacob's acknowledgement of his name and nature was the key to God changing his name and nature, the new nature that Esau would eventually meet and accept. This new nature is that of "Israel." "And [the angel] said, your name shall be called no more Jacob, but Israel; for as a prince you have power with God and with men and have prevailed" (Genesis 32:28). God through the man-angel accomplished his goal to change the nature of Jacob in "the time of Jacob's trouble" before Jacob meets his "trouble" personified, his brother whom he tricked. Thus, Jacob's trouble with his brother ended through the angel of God changing Jacob's name and nature. In other words the volatile encounter between Esau and the new man "Israel" was defused because when they did eventually come together Esau met "Israel" (prince with God) and not Jacob, the trickster. Also, before I develop the angel's name, who wrestled with Jacob, it is important to know that this principle of name and nature being changed applies to some in the Church of our Lord Jesus Christ. God has sent both "men of God," through apostles, prophets, evangelists, pastors, teachers, and literal "angels of God" to wrestle with God's disciples in our times of troubles in order to change our trickster nature. All we have to do is acknowledge our true nature and God will heal us. I will tell you an event that occurred to me in a dream one night.

Personal Experience-the Invisible Man

Around 1988 after I recommitted my life to the Lord Jesus two years earlier, in a dream, I saw an exceptionally large great eagle in flight high in the clouds. The color of the eagle was the color of the flag of the United States of America. As the eagle was flying, I heard the "sound" of thunder. As I continued to listen, the "sound" of the thunder became a "voice" of thunder. The voice of thunder continued, as I saw the eagle in majestic flight, with its large wings pushing through the heaven and the clouds. As the eagle pushed through the sky in flight, I heard the "voice" of thunder say, "Judgment, judgment, judgment..." As the vision continued, an invisible man, an angel, wrestled with me at the foot of the bed; and I knew if I did not let him go he would break my thigh (I was aware of Jacob's encounter. However, I did not consider that I was to acknowledge my name and nature), and thus, I let the angel go. However, the encounter was real; the vision of the great eagle; the repeated voice of thunder are also true.; and God did eventually change my nature to be more like his nature.

What is the Angel's Name

Now, with regards to the name of the angel, the same inquiry was made by Jacob that Manoah and his wife inquired when they encountered the angel (Judges 13:18). Jacob wanted to know the angel's name. And both angel's initial responses are the same. Both the angel in Judges chapter thirteen and the angel who Jacob encountered wanted to know why each person asked their name. The angel responded to Jacob, "why is it you ask after my name" (Genesis 32:29).

This reveals the heart of most humans, there is a desire to know our angels' names; and apparently God has limited the amount of names of angels to be revealed in this life. In this case with regards to the angel's name it appears to me that it is found in the name Jacob gave to the place where the encounter happened. Jacob named the place "Peniel," the "face of God," because Jacob was convinced that he saw "God face to face," with an emphasis on both "God" and "face" (Genesis 32:30).

However, Jacob saw God's face in the face of the angel; hence the angel either revealed his name to Jacob as "the face of God," Peniel; or the name of the angel can be understood as "Peniel" due to the name Jacob gave the place of the wrestling. It is also worthy to note that the Hebrew word for "face" means to "turn" to someone or something. God's face in the face of the angel "turned" Jacob from trickster to Israel, a prevailing prince with God. In addition, as the land of Israel is now named after the person Jacob, so the place "Peniel" is named after the living God and the angel Peniel.

Note in Hosea chapter twelve, verse three, we learn that "in [Jacob's] strength, he struggles **with** ["et" (את)] God;" however the phrase used in Hosea chapter twelve, verse four stating, "he struggled **with** the Angel," is not the same word used in Hosea chapter twelve, verse three, for **"with."** The word **"with"** in Hosea chapter twelve, verse four can also be translated "he struggled **with-God angel** and prevailed." The Hebrew word translated as **"with"** is **"El (אֵל),"** the same Hebrew word translated as **"God [El (אֵל)]"** throughout the Bible.

And yes, Jacob was completely convinced his experience was with "the face of God" (Genesis 32:30); however, he also concluded that the experience was with an "angel" (Genesis 48:16). Thus, it can be concluded that as "Michael" was gifted to be "who-as-God," and "Gabriel" was gifted with the "might of God," it is possible the angel of God who encountered Jacob was gifted with the "face of God;" hence his name "Peniel." Yet, at this juncture, I would like to emphasize that naming the angel that wrestled with Jocob at "Peniel" is this author's understanding based on the context of the scriptures referencing Jacob's experience. So, with regards to this angel's name every person must be persuaded of God in their own mind (compare Romans 14:5).

Abaddon, the Angel of the Abyss

*Revelation 9:11, NASB: They have as **king** over them, **the angel of the abyss**; his name in Hebrew is **Abaddon**, and in the Greek he has the name **Apollyon**.*

One of the other names of an angel mentioned in the Bible is "king Abaddon." Abaddon" also known as "Apollyon" is called "the angel of the abyss." The abyss is the place where demons dread to go. The abyss is where Jesus was raised out of Death. The abyss is the place where Satan was judged to be imprisoned for a thousand years. The abyss is the place "the beast" in Revelation chapters thirteen and seventeen walked up from to rule for the three and a half years. The "**pit** of the abyss" is the place where the locust-scorpions ascended from to "torment" some of humanity for five months. Thus, this angel of the abyss "kingship" has to be developed from all these perspectives. First, let us develop his name. "Abaddon" or "Apollyon" by definition means destroyer, one who causes to perish, to ruin, to cut off permanently. Thus, Jesus has made Abaddon king of destruction. And the scriptures make it clear that demons and even Satan do not want to have anything to do with the abyss and this angel, Abaddon.

Abaddon, King of the Abyss

The angel Abaddon was introduced as a king in Revelation chapter nine during the Fifth (5th) Trumpet. During this trumpet, a star who previously fell from heaven into the earth was given the key to the "**pit** of the abyss" (Revelation 9:1) Note: the key the star had was to the "**pit** of the abyss" and not necessarily the key to all of the abyss, as the angel who bound Satan with the great chain in Revelation chapter twenty, verse one had the "key to the abyss." Thus, the star opened the pit of the abyss and out of the pit came locusts with scorpion tails.

Abaddon's Tormenting Locust-scorpions

These locust-scorpions were not the usual locusts or scorpions. They were like horses (fearless, strong and huge); they have "victor's crowns," (they will be successful in their assignment); they have the faces of men (sinful men will see themselves in their faces); they have hair like women (they are submitted to God's command through king Abaddon), they have teeth like lions (their teeth are used to bite and hold their prey), the have chest of iron (their chest protected them with the strength of iron); and tails with stings like scorpions (the tools that is used to hurt those who do not have God's seal in their forehead)—see Revelation 9:7-10. Also, unlike the natural locusts who have no king, these beasts have a king, Abaddon, the "Destroyer" (Proverbs 30:27, Revelation 9:11). These locusts must obey their king's rulership (Revelation 9:4).

With that said, the torment through Abaddon and his locust-scorpions was so severe that humanity came to the place to prefer death over the torment. However, for the first time "Death shall flee from them" (Revelation 9:6). Yes, Death who takes pleasure in killing, will flee from people seeking to die. This truth brings me to the next angel related to the Abyss, Death, because Death is a different angel from Abaddon.

Death and the Abyss

When the place of wisdom was being sought, "Abaddon and Death say, 'With **our** ears **we** have heard a report of it'" (Job 2822). Thus, even though the angel named Death is associated with the abyss, he is not Abaddon.

*Romans 10:6-7, NASB: 6But the righteousness that comes from faith speaks like this: Do not say in your heart, "Who will go up to heaven?" That is, to bring Christ down 7or, "Who will go down into the **abyss?**" That is, to bring Christ up from **the dead."**

Even though Death and Abaddon are indeed different angels, Death is also associated with the abyss as the Spirit of Jesus revealed through the Apostle Paul. When Jesus died he descended into the abyss into the chambers related to death. In Proverbs chapter seven, verse twenty-seven, when speaking of the harlot, the scripture says, "Her house is the way to **Sheol,** descending to the **chambers of death.** Thus, it can be concluded that the chambers in Sheol, the Hebrew equivalent of "Hell," relates to Death in the abyss. Revelation chapter twenty, verse thirteen makes it clear that the dead who do not belong to Jesus Christ are held in Death and Hell. In addition, after God resurrected Jesus from the pains of death out of the abyss, Jesus now "have the keys of hell and death" (Revelation 1:18, Acts 2:24, Romans 10:6-7)). In other words, as there is a key to a particular "pit" in the abyss that the star used to release the locust-scorpions, there is also a "key' to Death whose chambers are in the abyss; and there is a key to hell, who is also in the abyss. Yet, Abaddon is the apparent king over the entire abyss, with Jesus having all the keys related to the abyss.

Demons Spurn the Abyss

*Luke 8:26-30, NASB: [27]And when He had come out onto the land, He was met by a certain man from the city who was possessed with demons ... [28]And seeing Jesus, he cried out and fell before Him, and said in a loud voice, "What do I have to do with You, Jesus, Son of the Most High God? I beg You, **do not torment me"** .... [31]And they were entreating Him not to command them to depart into the **abyss.***

Abaddon, the Destroyer" is king over the abyss; and pursuant to reading the scriptures, Luke chapter eight, verses twenty-seven through thirty above, one can clearly see that "demons" consider the "abyss" a place of "torment" for them. That is, they fully understand the tormenting capabilities of the locust-scorpions Abaddon commands. In Revelation chapter

41

nine, verse five we learn that Abaddon's locust-scorpions "torments" with stings. In Luke chapter eight, verses twenty-seven through thirty, we see that this "torment" in the" abyss" is true also for "demons" once Jesus or Jesus' saints sends these demons to the abyss. That is, in Luke chapter eight, verses twenty-seven through thirty and Matthew chapter eight, verses twenty-nine, when Jesus cast out the demons from the man, they begged him not to "torment" them "before time" by sending them to the abyss **before time**.

Demons and their prince Satan are afraid of the type of torments the creatures in the abyss dishes out; to include but is not limited to the flux of flames. Therefore, they are in no rush to be sent to the abyss. The Book of Job also gave a glimpse of the underworld that is not very pleasant. Job calls the underworld a land "without order and where the light is as darkness" (Job 10:21-22).

There is no order in the underworld in hell, which is also adjacent to Abraham's bosom, in the sense that whoever goes there has no peace from torment, no set time to be tormented (compare Jesus' revealed knowledge of this place in Luke chapter sixteen, verses twenty-three through twenty-five). The torment in the underworld is without arrangement or permission; and it is so dark in the underworld that even what may be considered as "light" is "gloom."

By the way, the "time" will come when Satan and his angels (demons (frog-like, monkey-like, fowl-like) serpents, dragons, scorpions, etcetera) will be bound in the abyss to be tormented before they are eventually sent to the eternal fire for eternal punishment (Matthew 25:41-46, Revelation 19:20, Revelation 20:10)! This same fear is apparently true for Satan.

Satan, and Demons Spurns the Abyss

Luke 8:26-30, NASB: ²⁷*And when He had come out onto the land, He was met by a certain man from the city who was possessed with demons … *²⁸*And seeing Jesus, he cried out and fell before Him, and said in a loud voice, "What do I have to do with You, Jesus, Son of the Most High God? I beg You, **do not torment me"** …. *³¹*And they were entreating Him not to command them to depart into the* **abyss.**

Revelation 20:1-3, NASB: ¹*And I saw an angel coming down from heaven, having **the key of the abyss** and a great chain in his hand.* ²*And he **laid hold of** the dragon, the serpent of old, who is the devil and Satan, and bound him for a thousand years, *³***and threw him into the abyss,** and shut it and sealed it over him, so that he should not deceive the nations any longer, until the thousand years were completed; after these things he must be released for a short time.*

In Luke chapter eight, verses twenty-seven through thirty, the demons exposed concerning themselves that they spurn the abyss and the torments meted out in the abyss. Likewise, their ruling angel, Satan, also spurns the abyss. This is seen in Revelation chapter twenty, verses one through three coupled with Revelation chapter twelve, verse twelve and Matthew chapter eight verse twenty-eight. In Revelation twelve, the great Michael and his angels fought against the great dragon and his angels. The great dragon and his angels "were not strong enough" to withstand the force of Michael and his angel.

Thus, the dragon and his angels were cast out of heaven; and we learned from this event that the Devil knew he now had a "short time" (Revelation 12:12). One of the things related to this "short time" is connected to what the legion of demons exposed in Luke, chapter eight, and Matthew chapter eight. Per the Apostle Matthew's account, the demons insisted that if Jesus sent them to the abyss, it would have been "before time" "And behold, they cried out, saying, "What do we have to do with You, Son of God? Have You come here to **torment us before the time** (Matthew 8:29, NASB)? Thus, they asked Jesus to rather send them into the swine instead of the abyss. However, Revelation chapter twelve, verse twelve makes it clear that the "before time" is now turned into a "short time," (i.e., 3 ½ years).

It follows that in Revelation chapter twenty, verses one through three, the "short time" had expired and the great dragon, Satan was bound and sent to the abyss for one thousand years. However, the description of Satan being bound and sent to the abyss also reveals that all Satan(s) spurns the abyss. In the language of Revelation chapter twenty, verses one through three, Satan had to be "laid hold of."

This Greek word translated as "laid hold of" is better defined as to "use strength," "to govern" or "to control." Yes, the angel with the great chain had to use his strength to govern the great dragon. In other words, it was a fight because demons and angels who did not stand in the Truth spurn the abyss and king Abaddon. In addition, the angel who had the great chain must have been one of God's strongest angels; because even though he had the chain in one of his hand, he was "strong enough" to govern the great dragon, bind him with the great chain and then threw the great dragon in to the abyss; and this same angel also "sealed" the abyss after the dragon was bound in the abyss to be tormented for one thousand years; after which, Satan is eventually be sent to the lake of fire eternally!

Tartarus

*2 Peter 2:4, BLB: For if God did not spare the angels having sinned, but having cast them down to **Tartarus**, in chains of gloomy darkness, delivered them, being kept for judgment.*

In closing of this chapter, we will discuss a place of gloom called Tartarus. There are some angels whose sin merited the punishment of being "sent to the deepest abyss of Hades (Hell), called "Tartarus." Per the Apostle Peter these angels were "sent to Tartarus," bound in the chains of gloomy darkness. That is not only were they locked up in the deepest abyss of Hell; they were also bound in "chains of 'zophos'" — gloomy darkness — where they live in gloom and darkness until the day of judgment.

That is, in addition to the chains being chains, "zophos," gloom-darkness, itself, is also the chain these angels who sinned experience daily, until the day of judgment according to Jude chapter one, verse six. These are the angels that apparently cohabitated with humans,[7] a sin so unacceptable to God that any angel who participates in this type of sin is bound speedily, placed in the deepest Hell, "Tartarus," and not allowed to continue interaction with any angel or human until their final punishment. With that said, **"Tartarus"** is defined as: the netherworld, the place of punishment fit only for demons. Later, Tartarus came to represent eternal punishment for wicked people. Tartarus is a Greek name for the underworld, especially the abode of the damned, it also means to send into the subterranean abyss reserved for demons and the dead. In Greek mythology, Tartarus was a "place of punishment under the earth, to which, for example, the Titans were sent" (Souter). Strong's defined Tartarus is from Tartarus (the deepest abyss of Hades).

---

[7] This truth will be developed later in this book.

Apsinthos, the Great Star

Revelation 8:10-11: [10]*And the third angel sounded, and there fell **a** **great star** from heaven, burning as it were a lamp, and it fell upon the third part of the rivers, and upon the fountains of waters;* [11]*And the name of the **star is called Wormwood:** and the third part of the waters became wormwood; and many men died of the waters, because they were made bitter.*

In the Book of the Revelation of Jesus Christ, a great star is named. This "star's" name is translated as "Wormwood" in English; but as "Apsinthos" in the Greek language. "Apsinthos" is described as "bitter;" and is defined as "undrinkable," or bitterness. Every star has a name (Psalm 147:4). Therefore, all the stars that are personified in the Book of the Revelation of Jesus Christ have a name, including the star in Revelation chapter nine, verse one. With that said, let us establish how this "star" can be interpreted as an angel before I describe its works of Apsinthos.

Jesus Defined Stars as Angels

*Revelation 1:20, NKJV: The mystery of the seven stars which you saw in My right hand, and the seven golden lampstands: **The seven** **stars are the angels of the seven churches,** and the seven lampstands which you saw are the seven churches.*

The Lord Jesus, himself, stated that the "seven stars" in his right hand are "seven angels of the seven Churches.." It follows that stars can be interpreted to mean angels in certain contexts. However, you, the readers, have to decide if you agree with my interpretation or not that this "great star," Apsinthos, is an angel called Apsinthos. In the Fifth Trumpet, the star who also fell from heaven seems to be personified. The "star" in Revelation chapter nine, verse one was given a "key to the pit abyss" which means that this "star" is not a planet. The star is a being who can hold a key.

46

The star is a great spirit angel or a great angel of the Churches who fell. Therefore, it appears to me the "great star," Apsinthos, can prophetically speak of a literal star that will fall upon the various sources of water in the earth and make them bitter. This "great star," Apsinthos, also represents a literal great spirit angel and/or great human messengers (plural), who will release bitter words to people through their messaging, and these preachers are themselves bitter. In this context, let us look at the scriptures for interpretation comparing spiritual things with spiritual things (1 Corinthians 2:13-16).

Burning as a Lamp

*Revelation 8:10: And the third angel sounded, and there fell **a great star** from heaven, **burning as it were a lamp** ....*

*Isaiah 62:1: For Zion's sake will I not hold my peace, and for Jerusalem's sake I will not rest, until the righteousness thereof go forth as brightness, **and the salvation thereof as a lamp that burns**.*

If we interpret Revelation chapter eight, verse ten literally, and we can, then there will be a great star, Apsinthos that falls to the earth from the heaven burning as a lamp. Picture a meteorite burning as a light when it enters the earth's atmosphere. With that said, this "great star" can also represent a "great" angel, named Apsinthos who will fall on one third of the rivers and fountains of water pretending to bring "salvation." Because this great star "burns as it were a lamp;" and Isaiah said that "salvation" is "as a lamp that burns." That is, this great star angel will look like it is bringing salvation through words depicted by the phrase "fountain of waters;" however, its nature is "bitter" and "undrinkable.

Per the Apostle James "fountain of water" is equated to "words" people speak with their tongues. Thus, the star falling on the fountain of water represents words that will be undrinkable because the water is made bitter. Per Apostle James, the words by the tongue can be both bitter water and sweet water. In the case of the great star, Apsinthos, the water became bitter and not sweet.

Embittered Fountains of Water

*Revelation 8:10: And the third angel sounded, and there fell **a great star** from heaven, burning as it were a lamp, and it fell upon **the third part of the rivers**, and upon the **fountains of waters**.*

*James 3:8-11:⁸But the **tongue** can no man tame; it is an unruly evil, full of deadly poison. ⁹Therewith bless we God, even the Father; and therewith curse we men, which are made after the similitude of God. ¹⁰Out of the **same mouth** proceeds **blessing and cursing**. My brethren, these things ought not so to be. ¹¹Does a **fountain** send forth at the same place **sweet water and bitter?***

We see that Apostle James equated "water fountains" to words we speak. It follows that Apsinthos will fall on the tongues of men and they will be releasing **bitterness** (cursing) to one third of humanity; and this bitter water will kill. Saying it another way, a great star, called Apsinthos, understood to be an angel per one of Jesus' definitions of "stars" will influence bitterness in preachers and they will embitter others. This truth that the bitterness of one person can cause trouble for others is descriptive of spurious sons in the Book of Hebrews.

*Hebrews 12:15: Looking diligently lest any man fail of the grace of God; lest any root of **bitterness** springing up trouble you, and thereby **many be defiled**.*

The bitterness of one can defile others. The bitterness of the great star Apsinthos, can embitter one-third of humanity and kill one-third of humanity. That is, when God's people sit under bitter preachers who have been embittered by Apsinthos, their bitterness will both kill and embitter others.

This is why it is especially important that the people of God should not remain bitter all their lives and embitter others. We must allow the "tree" of Jesus Christ to heal our waters. We must learn to "forgive everyone for everything."

Embittered Rivers

*Revelation 8:10: And the third angel sounded, and there fell **a great star** from heaven, burning as it were a lamp, and it fell upon **the third part of the rivers**, and upon the **fountains of waters**.*

Again, the great star Apsinthos, an angel, also embittered the "rivers." Thus, as with the fountain of waters, so with the rivers.; a great star will fall out of heaven into the rivers and embitter one-third of the rivers on earth. If I am alive when this happens, I don't look forward to that day. This embittering of the rivers and fountains will occur in the Third Trumpet. With that said, what is the spiritual application to the angel Apsinthos embittering the rivers of waters. "Rivers" is translated from the Greek word "potamos" (think of the name of the Potomac river on the east coast).

"Potamos" is from root "pino" to drink. Hence, "rivers" speak of any water that people or animals can drink. Thus, bitterness will be the drink available through one-third of the water of words offered in the earth. And don't misunderstand, this bitterness will appear sweet to some of those who imbibe this water. Proverbs twenty-seven, verse seven says **"to the hungry soul every bitter thing is sweet."** Thus, there will be a time on the earth, and now is, when the soul of humanity will be so thirsty that they will drink even the bitter rivers offered by bitter preachers under the influence of the bitter star. They will be drinking this bitterness thinking it will bring sweetness to their lives; however, there is death in the liquids.

Bitter Water Kills

Revelation 8:10-11: 10And the third angel sounded, and there fell a great star from heaven, burning as it were a lamp, and it fell upon the third part of the rivers, and upon the fountains of waters; 11And the name of the star is called Wormwood: and the third part of the waters became wormwood; and **many men died of the waters, because they were made bitter.**

James 3:14-16: 14But if you have **bitter envy** *and* **self-seeking** *in your hearts, do not boast and lie against the truth. 15This wisdom does not descend from above, but is* **earthly, sensual (lit., soulish), demonic.** *16For where envy and self-seeking exist, confusion and every evil thing are there.*

The Apostle James said that "bitterness," "envy" and "strife" related to electioneering is "earthly," "demonic" and "soulish." Thus, any form of bitterness is demon-like. In other words, demons are bitter spirits. Any form of wisdom that is not pleasant to the senses is demonic. Esau's embittered his parents "spirits" and eventually bitterness caused him to lose his birthright, per the writer of the Book of Hebrews.

The phrase "grief of mind" in Genesis chapter twenty-six, verse thirty-five is literally "bitterness of spirit" when speaking of Esau marriage to women[8] who did not serve the God of Abraham (Genesis 26:34-35, Hebrews 12:15-17). In addition, the angel revealed to John in Revelation chapter eight that the bitterness caused by the great star Apsinthos, kills. "Men **died** of the waters because the waters were made bitter." Thus, there exist bitter preachers, bitter shamans, bitter believers, and so on who are under the influence of

---

[8] Note: per the scriptures, God is not prejudiced against mixed marriage, God is against his people (the Church) marrying unbelievers who worship other gods. Saints are encouraged to marry believers in the Lord Jesus, with no reference to race (1 Corinthians 7, Ruth, etc.).

Apsinthos embittering the world unto death. Yet, there is a person and the Way that is able to heal bitterness.

Jesus' Tree Heals Bitter Water

1 Peter 2:24: **Who (Jesus)** *Himself bore our sins in His own body* **on the tree,** *that we, having died to sins, might live for righteousness –* **by whose stripes you were healed.**

Exodus 15:22-25: *²²So Moses brought Israel from the Red sea …* *²³And when they came to Marah, they could not drink of* **the waters of Marah, for they were bitter:** *therefore the name of it was called* **Marah.** *²⁴And the people murmured against Moses, saying, What shall we drink? ²⁵And he cried unto the LORD; and the LORD* **showed him a tree,** *which* **when he had cast into the waters, the waters were made sweet:** *there he made for them a statute and an ordinance, and there he proved them, ²⁶And said, If you will diligently hearken to the voice of the LORD your God, and wilt do that which is right in his sight, and will give ear to his commandments, and keep all his statutes, I will put none of these diseases upon thee, which I have brought upon the Egyptians: for I am the LORD that heals you.*

Moses and the people in the wilderness came to a place called "Marah" because the water there was bitter and undrinkable. However, when Moses sought the Lord for a solution, the Lord directed Moses to take a "tree" and throw it in the water and the "tree" would "heal" the water and make it "sweet." This miracle, the Lord showed to the children of Israel in the wilderness, points to the healing from bitterness the heavenly Father offers to all humanity through the "tree" that Jesus was crucified on. As the "tree" Moses tossed into the bitter water sweetened the water, so the "tree" Jesus was hanged on released "healing," to us, when we apply the "cross" to any bitterness we may have experienced in life. As the Apostle Peter said, "by Jesus' wounds we were healed." Yes, there is healing for all manner of sickness, including but not limited, to bitterness. **That is, the tree of Jesus (the cross of Christ)**

protects his disciples from Apsinthos. How does this tree of the Lord Jesus work on our behalf to heal our bitter waters? We have to forgive all for all sins they may have sinned against us as Jesus also forgave his crucifers. While Jesus was on the cross he refused to accept the bitterness, the wine mixed with bitterness, they offered him (Matthew 27:34, John 19:26). We also must resist any cloaking of bitterness cloaked in wine. In addition, Jesus did eventually drink the bitterness just before he died.

That is, Jesus not only rejected bitterness, but he also absorbed the bitterness they offered him on the cross, as he also forgave their sins. During Jesus' pain of the bitter cross, Jesus chose not to be bitter against those who unjustly crucified him. Instead, he absorbed their bitterness and forgave them. Jesus said, "Father forgive them for they know not what they do" (Luke 23:34a). So, as we also must forgive others of any bitter experience caused by them, and God will supernaturally also heal us by also forgiving us of our sins (Matthew 6:14). There is "sweet" healing in God's forgiving us through the tree (cross) of Christ!

King Angels and their Thrones

*Colossians 1:16, NASB: For by Him all things were created, both in the heavens and on earth, visible and **invisible**, whether **thrones** or dominions or rulers or authorities — all things have been created through Him and for Him.*

In the scriptures, it is clear that there are "angels of the Lord" and "angels of God;" just as the Word of God also makes it clear that there are prophets of the Lord as opposed to prophets of the people or prophets of Baal. It follows that there are unseen king angels and unseen "thrones" who are not the Lord's in the sense that they "stood not in the Truth" or they did not "remain in the Truth" (John 8:44). Kings sit upon "thrones;" and there exist many **king angels** as exemplified in one of our previous discussions of king Abaddon.

The Church has thought that Satan is the only king angel in the authority of darkness. However, be reminded that there exists **king death, and kings of Persia** (Daniel 10:13). There is also **king leviathan** (Job 41:1; 34); and **king Heylel, the spirit king of Babylon** (Isaiah 14). They are among the kings in the unseen realm. Satan himself has "seven heads" who wore "crowns" referred to in Revelations. These "crowns" are literally "diadems," ruling crowns, not "stephanos," a victor's crown.

*Revelation 12:3: And there appeared another wonder in heaven; and behold a great red dragon, having **seven heads** and ten horns, and **seven crowns** upon his heads.*

Satan holds or controls these heads. It is also significant to know that kings wear "crowns." Therefore, these "heads" have "crowns" and they represent seven kings of Satan. In the Book of Hebrews, we learn that Satan "had" **(lit., held)** the power of death (Hebrews 2:14). This truth also demonstrates why Satan is also called Prince of **demons** (Matthew 12:24). Satan "had"(past tense) the "government-strength" of death, but Jesus **now** holds the keys of death and hell (Revelation 1:18). However, death is still a king angel, whose power Satan uses until Satan and all his angels, Death and Hell, etcetera is cast into the lake of fire, the Second Death (Revelation 20:10; 20:14).

King Death

The angel of death rules in the areas of death, plagues, hunger, famine, the sword, the wild beasts of the earth, **terror,** pains of death, etcetera. Death is a king because he is called the **"king** of terrors" in Job chapter eighteen. In the Book of Job, the writer talks about king death in relation to the fate of the wicked. Even though Job's friends were wrongly calling him wicked, there is truth in their statements, even as the Apostle Paul also quoted one of their statements as true in Romans chapter eleven, verse thirty-three from Job chapter eleven verse seventeen. Therefore, in the context of this teaching, their statement is true especially concerning the angelic realm. They declared Death to be related to hunger, terror, calamity, destruction and so on.

Job 18:11-14: **11Terrors** *shall make him afraid on every side and shall drive him to his feet.* *12His strength shall be* **hunger-bitten,** *and destruction shall be ready at his side.13It shall devour the strength of his skin: even the* **firstborn of death** *shall devour his strength.* *14His confidence shall be rooted out of his tabernacle, and it shall bring him to the* **king of terrors.**

The writer in Job uses words like, "the firstborn of death" (part of which is terror) "hunger bitten" one of the workings of the angel named Death; and the **"king of terrors"** (death himself). Note: One of the many deliverance our Lord Jesus accomplished for his brothers (the Church) is Jesus "freed those who through **fear of death** were subject to slavery all their lives" (Hebrews 2:14-15). As one can see, king death sits enthroned upon these things; yet he is now subjected to Jesus Christ and Jesus' disciples. It is still true though that Death still uses these things against humanity.

*Revelation 6:8: And I looked and behold a pale horse: and **his name** that sat on him was **Death, and Hell** followed with him. And power was given unto them over the fourth part of the earth, to kill with **sword,** and with **hunger,** and with **death (or plague),** and with the **beasts** of the earth.*

Per the text above, we see that Death is enthroned over the sword, hunger (famine), plagues, and over the beasts of the earth, terror, etcetera. With that said, let us also look at a beast called "king leviathan.

King Leviathan

*Job 41:1; 34, NASB: ¹"Can you draw out **Leviathan** with a fishhook? Or press down his tongue with a cord? ... ³⁴"He looks on everything that is high; He is **king over all the sons of pride."***

*Job: 3:8, NASB: Let those curse it who curse the day, Who are **prepared to rouse Leviathan.***

*Psalms 74:14, NASB: You crushed the **heads of Leviathan;** You gave him as food for the creatures of the wilderness.*

*Psalms 104:26, NASB: There the ships move along, [And] **Leviathan,** which You have formed to sport in it.*

*Isaiah 27:1, NASB: In that day, the LORD will punish **Leviathan the fleeing serpent,** with His fierce and great and mighty sword, even **Leviathan the twisted serpent;** And He will kill the **dragon** who [lives] in the sea.*

Leviathan is used six (6) times in the Bible; and since six (6) is a number that relates to "mankind," we should not be ignorant of this Leviathan. It appears there is a literal Leviathan in the sea; and there is a spiritual Leviathan in the sea of humanity. In Job chapter forty-one, verse thirty-four,

Leviathan is called a "king." However, he is king over all the "sons of pride," those who strut about like a pride of lions. Job chapter three, verse eight makes it clear that only those who are "prepared" can "rouse Leviathan." In other words, when one reads God's description of Leviathan in Job chapter forty-one, it takes the power of God to subdue this dragon; and a person must be of genuine birth in Christ to take on any demons least these dragons traumatize the powerless (Acts 19:13-17).

In addition, this king Leviathan's breath burns so powerful that it burns under water (Job 41:19-21). The eyes of this dragon are like the eyelids of the dawn (Job 41:18). Does this mean that in the darkness of the deep sea, if one were to see him, his eyelids would be like dawn in the darkness? Leviathan is also stated as having "heads."

If these heads are literal, then this dragon has more than one head. However, since Leviathan is also a spiritual entity, the heads may refer to the seven heads of the great dragon Satan. Finally in Isaiah, Leviathan is called a "serpent" hence he is apparently among the serpents Jesus called our enemies (Luke 10: 17-20). He is called a "fugitive" fleeing from God; however, he will eventually be caught (Revelation 20:1-3). He is also called twisted or crooked serpent, which again, tells of his nature' and he is also only king over sons of pride! Therefore, it behooves all believers to renounce pride in any form. There are benefits in a humble state by submitting to the living God. In our submission to the living God, the Devil must flee from us when we resist him (James 4:6-7).

Rahab, the Sea Dragon

Psalms 89:8-10, NASB: *⁸O LORD God of hosts, who is like You, O mighty LORD? Your faithfulness also surrounds You. ⁹You rule the swelling of the **sea;** when its waves rise, You still them. ¹⁰You Yourself crushed **Rahab** like one who is slain; you scattered Your enemies with Your mighty arm.*

*Isaiah 51:9, NASB: Awake, awake, put on strength, O arm of the LORD; awake as in the days of old, the generations of long ago. Was it not You who cut **Rahab** in pieces, who pierced the **dragon.***

*Job 9:13, NASB: "God will not turn back His anger; beneath Him crouch the **helpers** of **Rahab.***

*Job 26:12, NASB: "He quieted the sea with His power, and by His understanding He shattered **Rahab.***

There is Rahab, the dragon of the sea. He rages in the sea demonstrated when the waves thereof arise. There is one who controls this controller of the sea though! His name is Jesus. In Luke chapter eight, verses twenty-four and twenty-five, Jesus encountered the raging of the sea and by Jesus' powerful words of faith, calmed the raging sea. Yes, Psalm eighty-nine says, "You rule the raging of the sea: when the waves thereof arise, you still them. You have **broken Rahab in pieces**, as one that is slain; you have scattered your enemies with your strong arm." Jesus breaks Rahab and silences him in the sea.

Rahab is also the spirit that ruled Egypt both literal Egypt and spiritual Egypt. And according to Job chapter nine, verse thirteen, Rahab also has "helpers" under him as Satan has angels subjected to him. Thus, Rahab is a dragon prince that ruled Egypt with his helpers. In Revelation chapter eleven, there is a place identified as "spiritually called Sodom and Egypt." Thus, there is also spiritual Egypt ruled by Rahab. This spirit of Egypt is the dragon that rules in the sea of humanity over people who walk in the practices of Egypt to include, but limited to, the practices of powers of sorcery ascertained from Rahab as displayed by Jannes and Jambres who withstood Moses with their sorcery.

*Revelation 11:8, NKJV: And their dead bodies will lie in the street of the great city which **spiritually** is called Sodom and **Egypt**, where also [c]our Lord was crucified.*

*Isaiah 30:1; 7: NASB: [1]"Woe to the rebellious children," declares the LORD, "who execute a plan, but not Mine, and make an alliance, **but not of My Spirit,** in order to add sin to sin; [2]who proceed down **to Egypt** without consulting Me, to take refuge in the safety of Pharaoh and to seek shelter in the shadow of Egypt! .... [7]Even Egypt, whose help is vain and empty. Therefore, I have called her **"Rahab who has been exterminated."***

God called the dragon spirit that ruled Egypt, "Rahab;" and he also stated that Rahab was exterminated. The Hebrew word translated as exterminated is better translated as "to cease" (Strong's #7673). That is, God caused Rahab and her work to cease through the power and faith of our Lord Jesus Christ. Also, Job makes it clear that the "sea" and the "dragon" have a "watcher" angel to keep guard on this dragon.

Job chapter seven, verse twelve says, "Am I the sea or a **dragon** that you post a **watch** over me?" The sea and her "proud waves" have to be monitored (Job 38:11). The dragon of the sea, Rahab also has to be monitored. One of the reasons is "Rahab" is defined as "Storm," "to urge severely," "arrogance," etcetera. It follows that this storm dragon must be monitored by a watcher angel. In the Book of Revelation though, this spirit of Rahab will raise up again against the two witnesses, in some people who follows the beast, and resist the two witnesses as Jannes and Jambres resisted Moses and Aaron (2 Timothy 3:8, Revelation 11:8, Exodus 7:11, etc.). However, Jesus will have the final say. Jesus will send "Satan and his angels" to the lake of "eternal fire prepared for the Devil and his angels" (Matthew 25:41, Revelation 19:20, Revelation 20:10).

Satan's Seven Crowns

*Revelation 12:3, NASB: And another sign appeared in heaven: and behold, a great red dragon having **seven heads** and ten horns, and on his heads were **seven diadems.***

*Matthew 12:22; 24-26: 22Then was brought unto him one possessed with a devil, blind, and dumb: and he healed him, insomuch that the blind and dumb both spoke and saw.... 24But when the Pharisees heard it, they said, this fellow doth not cast out devils, but by **Beelzebub the prince of the devils.** 25And Jesus knew their thoughts, and said unto them, every kingdom divided against itself is brought to desolation; and every city or house divided against itself shall not stand: 26And **if Satan cast out Satan**, he is divided against himself; how shall then his kingdom stand?*

Jesus healed a person possessed by a demon. However, instead of the Pharisees rejoicing that a person had been healed, they began to blaspheme Jesus and the Holy Spirit in Jesus. In addition, Jesus' response was also insightful. In Jesus' response, he declared that "Satan" was in essence a corporate entity. That is, the angels and demons that follow Satan are also called "Satan." There is a difference between" "the Satan" himself and Satan (the corporate Satan). "The Pharisees ... said this fellow doth not cast out devils, but by **Beelzebub the prince of the devils."** Jesus responded by saying, **"and if Satan cast out Satan,** he is divided against himself; how shall his kingdom stand?" There is Satan the prince of demons; and there is Satan, the many angels under Satan. **This shows that there is a corporate Satan.** The corporate Satan is seen in Leviathan with its heads; as it is seen in the great dragon with its seven heads, ten horns and its tail. Our Lord Jesus also demonstrated this truth in the parable of the Sower.

*Mark 4:3-4; 15: ³Hearken; behold, there went out a Sower to sow: ⁴And it came to pass, as he sowed, some fell by the wayside, and the **fowls of the air** came and devoured it up.... ¹⁵And these are they by the wayside, where the word is sown; but when they have heard, **Satan** cometh immediately, and taketh away the word that was sown in their hearts.*

The **"fowls (plural) of the air"** are called **"Satan."** Thus, Satan is a corporate entity. In Revelation chapter twelve, we learn that "the great dragon, that 'original' serpent called the Devil and Satan" has seven heads and ten horns. It appears to me that the seven heads point to the corporate heads (king angels) that are also called Satan. Here is the list of the seven kings under Satan and that are kings angels with Satan (Ephesians 1:21, Ephesians 6:12, Colossians 1:16, 1 Peter 3:22, the orders are random).

The Great Dragon's Seven Heads:

1. Principalities, or beginnings, arch-princes ("Archas")
2. Authorities ("Exousias")
3. Powers ("Dynameos")
4. Cosmic-governments ("kosmoskratos")
5. Spiritual hurts upon heavens ("Ponerias)
6. Thrones ("Thronoi")
7. Lords ("Kyriotetes")

Note: among these seven heads, with seven crowns, and therefore seven king angels, Satan himself is also a "king," a "Lord" and a "glory." Hence, even though we are to indeed rebuke Satan in the name of the Lord Jesus, and God will indeed crush him under our feet, we are not to blaspheme him as Jesus, his creator, and Michael the archangel demonstrated to us how to carry ourselves (John 14:30, Jude 1:8-10, Joshua 3). With that said, Satan's kingship is also seen in what Peter called Satan's "oppression" in Acts chapter ten, verse thirty-eight, which is literally translated as "down-dynasty."

That is, the Apostle Peter declared that Satan "oppression" ("down-dynasty") was overruled (removed from the oppressed) through Jesus' anointing with the Holy Spirit and power. Per second Timothy chapter six verse fifteen, Jesus' "Pontentate" (lit., dynasty) is defined as Jesus being "King of kings and Lord of lords." In other words, Jesus' "dynasty" defines Jesus, the King who rules over other kings; and Jesus, the Lord, who is Lord over other lords.

In Acts chapter ten, verse thirty-eight, Satan is said to have a "down-dynasty" that is translated as "oppressed." Thus, Satan is a "king" oppressor over other "kings" who oppresses humanity. Satan is "lord" oppressor over other lords who oppresses humanity. In other words, his dynasty "downs" humanity into despair. However, Jesus' Dynasty supersedes all dynasties and heals the oppressed with his life-producing Spirit.

Nonetheless, we now see in Satan all the attributes of the seven heads of the Satanic conspiracy. Satan is himself an oppressive "king" (enthroned) dragon (Acts 10:38, 2 Timothy 6:15). He is also a "lord" dragon (Jude 1:8-10) . He is also a "beginning" prince or principality (John 14:30). He perverted his "authority" into unforgiveness (Acts 26:18). He is called the one who hurts (1 John 5:19, 1 John 3:12-15). He possesses powers and wonders of falsehood (2 Thessalonians 2:9). He is the beginning of this "kosmos" or world (John 14:30, John 12:31). And finally, he is also the "god of this age" who blinds people's mind from seeing the Light of the gospel of the glory of Christ" (2 Corinthians 4:3-6).

Brief Exposition of Satan's Seven King Angels

Principalities:

Principalities, beginnings, or "arch-princes" are angels who "begin" sins in humanity in an attempt to trap them in the things that oppose faith towards the living God and oppose the Truth. These beginnings are nullified through the mystery of Christ revealed in the nations. This mystery of Christ, briefly summed up, is that both believing Jews and believing Gentiles are now in one Body through Jesus Christ; and the Body of Christ is to be the exact representation of the glory of Christ to all as a corporate "son" – Ephesians 1 through Ephesians 3, Colossians 1, Galatians 3 through Galatians 4, etcetera.

Authorities

Authorities relate to angels who use their authority, like the "authority of the air" to energize some to be "unpersuadable" towards the Truth of God and to encourage hedonism related to things like the lust of the flesh and the lust of the mind. Satan also uses "authority" to persuade humanity that they cannot be forgiven of their sins; and these authorities works "in" their victims "I" (their existence). Satan uses the authorities who also did not stand in the writings of Truth to also deceive humans not to believe in all the facets of Truth concerning Jesus – Ephesians 2:1-3, Acts 26:18. Colossians 1:13.

Powers

Powers, or dynamic ability, or miraculous abilities relate to angels who were enthroned and now use their supernatural abilities illegally in humanity to deceive mankind that their power is indeed the power of God, when it is indeed inferior and false in relation to God's glorious power and God's Truth. These powers pose as God's power in direct opposition to the Truth of God – Acts 8:9-24, Revelation 13:11-15, Revelation 16:13-14.

"Kosmoskratos"

"Kosmoskratos" is the literal Greek reading of the phrase the "rulers ... of this word" in Ephesians chapter six, verse twelve. "Kosmoskratos" is better translated as "world-strength," "world-governments," "world-rule." "Kratos" is the the Greek word transliterated as "cratic;" and it is used in words like "democratic," or "people-rule." Thus, there are invisible "rulers" of the "world" orders who rule over kings (presidents, prime ministers, etc.). They do not have Jesus's Spirit as the ruling Spirit over their nations! These "kosmoskratos" do not stand in the Truth, following their leader Satan. In fact, there are "world-governments" of this darkness that is blinded to the gospel of the glory of Christ. — Ephesians 6:12, Ephesians 2:1-3, I John 4, 1 John 2:15-17, 2 Corinthians 4:3-6, etcetera.

Spiritual Hurts Upon-heavens

Spiritual hurts upon the heavens is an interesting sort that sometimes goes undetected. First one must understand that "spiritual" means "things of the spirit." Hence, these "spiritual hurts" relates to "spirits." In addition, the "hurts" occur in the heavens against the saints "who are seated with Christ in the 'upon-heavens.'" In other words, just because saints are seated in the heavenlies, does not mean we will not encounter unexplained hurts. That is, these thrones related to "spiritual hurts" are there to affect us. It is interesting that if all the Greek root words related to hurts ("poneria") are studied one will discover that the hurt of "poverty" and the hurt of one who toils in pain for daily bread are included in the definitions. That is, these spirits are set to impoverish us from all the "true" riches of God (especially God's ten spiritual riches) and bread (earthly and heavenly breads) afforded us through being joint-heir with our Lord Jesus Christ.

The Truth of God says, believers are indeed heirs of God's "true" riches, the riches of His glory (Romans 9:23); riches of His usefulness (Romans 2:4); riches of His grace (Ephesians 1:7); riches of His inheritance (Ephesians 1:18); riches of His understanding (Colossians 2:2); riches of His wisdom

(Romans 11:33); riches of His knowing (Romans 11:33); riches of His mercy (Ephesians 2:4); riches of His forbearing (self-restraint) — Romans 2:4; riches of His longsuffering (or long-to-anger) — Romans 2:4. However, with regards to spiritual hurts, we can see one of the reasons why Jesus included in the words we should pray to our "heavenly Father," is heavenly father gives us our "daily bread that comes upon us" and "deliver us from the hurtful." — Matthew 6:9-14, Ephesians 6:12, 1 John 3:12-15, 1 John 5:16.

Thrones

Thrones is exemplified in kingship as previously discussed, yet I will cite some other examples where Satan thrones wrestle against all believers through satanic doctrines. Jesus declared in Revelation chapter two verses twelve through seventeen that "Satan throne" was in a place called Pergamos; and Jesus revealed how this "throne" was affecting some of his saints at Pergamos. Pergamos by definition means "much marriage" (seen in the Greek word "per" and "gamos" marriage. That is, the practices related to the satanic "throne" of Pergamos includes but is not limited to "marring" every doctrine that is against God's holiness. The "throne" of Satan in this city martyred "Antipas" because "Antipas" was "against-all" ["anti" (against) and "pas" (all)] their immoral doctrines and idolatry. This satanic throne also propagated "the doctrine of Balaam" which is different from the "error of Balaam" and the "way of Balaam." The doctrine of Balaam consists of the doctrine of "the lie" which is direct opposition to God's Truth!

The "doctrine of Balaam" consists of the "counsel" of Balaam to Balak instructing Balak how to set sexually related traps against the sons of Israel (Numbers 31:16). And now Satan is using that same doctrine of instigating "fornication" and "intense fornication" in the Church at Pergamos. That is, in Numbers 25:1 of the Septuagint Old Testament Greek translation of Numbers chapter twenty-five, verse one, "whoredom" is translated as "ekporneusai" ("intense fornication) the same Greek word used only in the Book of Jude when he spoke of same-sexuality as practiced in Sodom and Gomorrah. Also, this satanic throne at Pergamos, preached the doctrine of the "Nicolaitans." This can mean that there was a doctrine related to leaders "dominating" Jesus' "laity" unto themselves (contrast 1 Peter 5:1-4). In other words, some false teachers "conquered" the "laity" to be subservient to Satan and his ministers.

With that said, Satan's throne is also exemplified through the throne of "the beast" and the "false prophet" who preaches worship of the beast and not Jesus as King. That is, it was the dragon, Satan who gave the beast his "seat," literally, "throne." This beast is a spirit from the abyss in a human king; and this beast is also a governmental system consists of principles related to the spirit of ancient Greece, the spirit of mystery Babylon, the spirit of Persia and the spirit of Rome (Revelation 13, Revelation 14:9-13, Revelation 17).

Lords

Lords is defined as dominion, controller, and properly means to exercise absolute ownership rights, or controlling rights. One of the ways these lord angels exercise these controlling rights is through the means of idolatry and/or serving idols. That is, Satan uses this throne to lord over people through false gods. In other words, entire nations are controlled by Satan who is behind their gods or multitude of demons also behind their idols.

*1 Corinthians 8:4-6, NASB: ⁴Therefore, concerning the eating of food sacrificed to **idols**, we know that an **idol is nothing** at all in the world, and that there is no God but one. ⁵For even if there are so-called **gods** whether in heaven or on earth, as indeed there are many gods and **many lords**, ⁶yet for us there is only one God, the Father,* *from whom are all things, and we exist for Him; and one Lord, Jesus Christ, by whom are all things, and we exist through Him.*

1 Corinthians 10:19-22, NASB: ¹⁹*What do I mean then? That a* **thing sacrificed to idols is anything,** *or that an idol is anything?* ²⁰*No, but I say that the things which the Gentiles* **sacrifice, they sacrifice to demons and not to God**; *and I do not want you to become sharers in demons.* ²¹*You cannot drink the cup of the Lord and* **the cup of demons;** *you cannot partake of the table of the Lord and the* **table of demons.** ²²*Or do we provoke the Lord to jealousy? We are not stronger than He, are we?*

Without getting into to many details, it is clear above in the scriptures that Paul associates the concept of nothing "idols" to "lords" and nothing idols to "gods." He also said that there are demons behind every idol. Hence, the **throne of lordship** is exercised over nations who worship demons, who worship the demons behind man-made or handmade idols, and so on (Revelation 9:20 with Revelation 9:13-21). However, there is another subtle form of idol worship that is called "covetousness." Covetousness is related to the idol of gain, which is falsely equated to godliness. Or covetousness related to the idol of greed also falls under the lord-throne of Satan, a controlling idol. In fact, one who is covetous, is a "idolater" one who" serves the idol" of gain.

Ephesians 5:5, NASB: For this you know with certainty, that no immoral or impure person or **covetous man, who is an idolater,** *has an inheritance in the kingdom of Christ and God.*

This type of idolatry has been occupying most of the Church since the days of the original Apostles of the Lamb and the Apostles of Christ until today. Some still teach the idolatrous gospel of Satan that says maturity is measured by the idolatry of what you own or gain. Some teach the false doctrine that the sign that you are "godly" is the abundance of gain you attain. These teachings are satanic lies; and in case you are not aware the result of satanic thoughts is also related to covetousness (2 Corinthians 2:11).

Luke 12:13-15, NASB: *[13]Someone in the crowd said to Him, "Teacher, tell my brother to divide the [family] inheritance with me." [14]But He said to him, "Man, who appointed Me a judge or arbitrator over you?" [15]Then He said to them, "Beware, and be on your guard against every form of* **greed (lit., covetousness); for not [even] when one has an abundance does his life consist of his possessions.**

2 Peter 3:1-3, NASB: *[1]But* **false prophets** *also arose among the people, just as there will also be* **false teachers** *among you, who will secretly introduce destructive heresies, even denying the Master who bought them, bringing swift destruction upon themselves. [2]Many will follow their sensuality, and because of them the way of the truth will be maligned; [3]and in [their]* **greed (lit., covetousness)** *they will* **exploit (or emporium)** *you with false words; their judgment from long ago is not idle, and their destruction is not asleep.*

1 Timothy 6:3-5; 11 NASB: *[3]If anyone advocates a* **different doctrine** *and does not agree with sound words, those of our Lord Jesus Christ, and with the doctrine conforming to godliness, [4]he is conceited [and] understands nothing; but he has a morbid interest in controversial questions and disputes about words, out of which arise envy, strife, abusive language, evil suspicions, [5]and constant friction between men of depraved mind and deprived of the truth,* **who suppose that godliness is a means of gain.** *[6]But godliness [actually] is a means of great gain when accompanied by contentment ....* **[11]But flee from these things, you man of God** ....

Angels Who Sinned

*2 Peter 2:4, BLB: For if God did not spare **the angels having sinned**, but having cast them down to Tartarus, in chains of gloomy darkness, delivered them, being kept for judgment.*

The apostle Peter made it very clear that there are "angels who sinned." Thus, as humans can sin so likewise angels. Yet, it was the angel Satan who apparently sinned first and then he seduced Adam and Eve to also sin. That is, per the beloved Apostle John, "the Devil sins from the beginning," before Adam and Eve sinned.

Satan sins from the Beginning

*1 John 3:8: He that commits sin is of the Devil; for the **Devil sins from the beginning**. For this purpose, **the Son of God was manifested**, that he might **destroy the works of the Devil**.*

"The Devil **sins** from the beginning" and "sin" became his "work." Thus, Jesus the Son of God was manifested to destroy this work of the Devil. The question must be asked, what is the "sin" the Devil committed in the beginning, before he also sinned against Adam and Eve and caused them to also sin.

The Apostle John defined this "sin" in first John chapter three verse three. In fact, the Apostle John exposed this type of sin related to not remaining in the Truth, in the previous chapter of first John chapter two, verses twenty through twenty-nine. With that said, first John chapter three, verse three, states that "everyone committing sin also commits lawlessness; and **sin is lawlessness.**

The sin of the Devil that John is referencing in first John chapter three, verse eight is the sin of lawlessness; and this lawlessness is explicitly defined in the Apostle Paul's epistle to the Thessalonians. Here is the Apostle Paul's definition that gives insight into the angel Satan sin from the beginning when Paul countered those who preach that the coming of the Lord is imminent; and Paul gave events that must occur before the Lord returns.

*2 Thessalonians 2:3-7a, NASB: 3Let no one in any way deceive you, for it will not come unless the apostasy comes first, and the **man of lawlessness** is revealed, the son of destruction, 4who **opposes and exalts himself above every so-called god or object of worship, so that he takes his seat in the temple of God, displaying himself as being God.** 5Do you not remember that while I was still with you, I was telling you these things? 6And you know what restrains him now, so that in his time he will be revealed. 7For the **mystery of lawlessness** is already at work ....*

The beloved Apostle John defined "sin is lawlessness." This "lawlessness" is defined by the Apostle Paul as a person "opposes and exalts himself above every so-called god or object of worship, so that he takes his seat in the temple of God, displaying himself as being God." Paul then said, this is the "mystery (secret) of lawlessness" that is "**already** at work." That is, in the beginning before Satan also sinned against God by "overreaching" against Adam and Eve, Satan sinned against Jesus. Satan opposed and exalted himself above Jesus and is still attempting to display himself as god. In other words, Satan's sin of lawlessness is that he instituted creature worshiping creatures, rather than standing in the Truth that created beings must worship the Creator. Jesus, the Christ, who taught the Apostles about the Devils' original sin of lawlessness, who was there at the beginning in his eternal state, gave us additional revelation of the Devil's lawlessness when he deliberated with the Jews who were resisting his doctrine related to Truth.

*John 8:44: You are of your father the Devil, and the lusts of your father you will do. He was **a murderer from the beginning,** and **abode not in the truth,** because there is no truth in him. When he speaks **'the lie,'** he speaks **'from'** his own: for he is a liar, and the father of it.*

69

Satan is a Murderer from the Beginning:

The Devil is a murderer from the beginning. This reveals one of the facets of lawlessness, opposing all that relates to the living God. In this case, the Devil murdered or "hated" the image of God in Jesus and in Adam and Eve. That is, the Devil is a "man-faced-slayer" from the beginning. With the understanding that in first John chapter three, verse fifteen "hate" is defined as "murder;" The Devil "hates" and would like to kill all who are "man-faced" (Jesus, the Son of God and humanity Jesus created). The Devil is also a "man-eyed-slayer," so the compound word for "murder" is literally translated from all its root words. Through Satan's overreaching and tempting both Adam and Eve, through their "sight," their spiritual sight was also affected. Adam and Eve, and thus all humanity, was separated from continuing to see and experience the garden of Eden, the third heaven, after they sinned. And to this day it is still difficult for humanity to see into the Spirit, into the third heaven. Thus, Satan killed our ability to see into the third heaven; however, Jesus has renewed our ability to see all that pertains to God and the heavens.

Satan Stood not in Truth and Fathered the lie:

Jesus also said that the Devil stood not in the truth. This understanding reveals the sin of lawlessness. Jesus is the Truth (John 14:6). The Spirit is the Truth (John 14:17). The Word of God is Truth (John 17:17). There is the "Word of Truth" or the "truth of the gospel," a gospel void of prejudices related to race, culture, a gospel not conflated with nationalism, pedigree, education, and money (Galatians 2:14, Ephesians 1:13, Ephesians 2, Ephesians 3, Galatians 3, etcetera). Equally as important, when the Devils "stood not in the truth" he lawlessly opposed all that relates to the Truth of Jesus being "King" (John 18:37). The Devil and his angels attempted and failed to exalt himself above the Kingship of Jesus. The Devil and his angels attempted to exalt themselves above the Spirit of Truth; and thus, the Devil fathered "the lie" of "speaking from his own self" and instituting creation worshiping and revering creation instead of creation worshiping and revering the Creator (Romans 1:22-26).

The Devil did not stand in the Word of Truth that is written; which "caused" truth not to be in him (John 8:44, Daniel 10:21). He lawlessly pits angels (now called Satan's angels) against Jesus; he pitted Adam and Eve against their Creator, the living God; he is pitting ethnics against ethnics, kingdom against kingdom, Christian against Christians, skin color against skin color, those who have money against those who do not have money. Thus, the angel Satan is sinning from the beginning **before** he caused Adam and Eve to sin.

"Shodim"

*Genesis 3:1: Now the serpent was more subtle than any **beast of the field** which the LORD God had made. And he said unto the woman, yes, has God said, you shall not eat of every tree of the garden?*

The serpent was "from" or "a part of" the "beast of the field." These "beast of the field" are different from the "beast of the earth" God created in Genesis chapter one, verse twenty-four. In Genesis chapter two, verses eighteen and nineteen, God created some additional "beast of the field," among whom was "the serpent," called the "original serpent," the great dragon, Satan, and the Devil in Revelation chapter twelve, verse nine. This truth that the original serpent was created after Adam, but before Eve is not unique to what the Lord Jesus has revealed to me. That is, the Septuagint (LXX), the Greek translation of the Old Testament of Genesis 2:19 states that "God created yet further" related to these second sets of beasts. Thus, God created further after Adam was created; and God created these beasts to "help" Adam before God "built" Eve from Adam's ribs. Yes, the first set of "help meet" was not Eve. The first set of "help meet" was the "beast of the field." However, Adam did not find a help meet among these beasts of the field. Therefore, God continued to create yet further by "building" Eve. The fact that Adam did not find any "help" among the newly created "beast of the fields" may hint to one of the reasons why Satan, overreached with his lies to tempt Eve. The serpent was apparently envious of the woman; because Adam rejected him and the other beasts of the field and chose his wife.

With that said, the Hebrew word and its associated root words for "field" is full of insight. The Hebrew word "shadeh" (שָׂדֶה) and its associated roots are translated as field, land, violence, ravage, destruction, burly, demon, breast, Almighty, to harrow a field, etcetera. These definitions are indeed very revealing. Was the "beast of the fields" originally created to also help Adam in the field? Is their ability to "destroy" or work "ruin" turned against mankind who they were to help originally?

Here is another compelling questions, was the serpent" created one of "shedim" (שֵׁדִים), or one of the demons? He is said to be "a part of" or "from" the beasts "of-the-field." (הַשָּׂדֶה). The Hebrew letter "hey" (ה) at the beginning of the word adds a definite article to the Hebrew word "shed," to make it "the shed." In addition, the use of the letter "hey" at the end of the word makes it feminine or "of" the "shed."

Therefore, the serpent is one of the beasts "of" the "shed." Using some of the definitions previously given in this section, the serpent was "of" those who "harrowed" the land, originally created to help Adam. The serpent was "of" the "burly" class, created brawny to help Adam subdue the earth. The serpent was "of" the "demon" class originally created not to be worshiped, but to "serve" Adam and Eve. Remember, God created "all" spirits, or "all" angels to "publicly-work" and "serve" the "heirs of salvation." The Hebrew word of angel, "malak" also means one who is deputized.

Thus, the angel Satan was originally deputized to help humanity. Originally, Adam, Eve and the serpent were not enemies in Satan's deputized role. The serpent could openly speak with Adam and Eve because he was not an enemy until after Satan caused Eve and Adam to fall, after God instituted enmity between them. In addition, Satan, the original serpent, was also known as the "prince of demons;" the "arch" "Satan" of the **corporate Satan (demons).** Therefore, he can be considered among the "shodim."

*Matthew 12:22-28: ²²Then one was brought to Him who was demon-possessed, blind and mute; and He healed him, so that the blind and mute man both spoke and saw. ²³And all the multitudes were amazed and said, "Could this be the Son of David?" ²⁴Now when the Pharisees heard it they said, "This fellow does not cast out demons except by **Beelzebub, the ruler of the demons.**" ²⁵But Jesus knew their thoughts and said to them: "Every kingdom divided against itself is brought to desolation, and every city or house divided against itself will not stand. ²⁶If Satan casts out Satan, he is divided against himself. How then will his kingdom stand? ²⁷And if I cast out demons by Beelzebub, by whom do your sons cast them out? Therefore, they shall be your judges. ²⁸But if I cast out demons by the Spirit of God, surely the kingdom of God has come upon you.*

*Hebrews 1:7; 1:12-14: ⁷And of the angels He says: "Who makes His angels spirits and His ministers a flame of fire" ... ¹³But to which of the angels have He ever said: "Sit at My right hand, till I make Your enemies Your footstool?" ¹⁴Are they not **all ministering (or public-working) spirits** sent forth **to minister (lit., serve)** for those who will inherit salvation?*

Other Spirits

In addition to God's myriads of holy and elect angels being called spirits, there are many other spirits of Satan who can be called "angels." In second Corinthians chapter twelve, verse seven we learn of an "angel of Satan" who God allowed to be a "thorn in Paul's flesh." In Revelation chapter twelve, verse seven, it is revealed again that there exists "Satan and his angels." And in second Corinthians chapter eleven, verse four , we see that Satan "is transformed"(outward "scheming") as "an angel of light."

All of Satan's angels and/or spirits are also subjected to the living God, even though Satan still overreaches at times (1 Peter 3:22, Luke 10:17-19, Job 1:6-12, Job 2:1-6, etc.). With that said, the "spirit of Python," (Ascertainer) is a beast spirit (Acts 16:6). There are seducing spirits (1 Timothy 4:1, 1 John 4:6). There is the "spirit of Antichrist," which is the same as the "another beast," and "the false prophet" in the Book of Revelation (1 John 4:1-3, Revelation 13:11; 16:13; 19:20).

There is the spirit of the world (1 Corinthians 2:12). The spirit prince of the authority of the air is also an archangel (Ephesians 2:1-3). The beast from the abyss is a spirit beast (Revelation 11:7; 17:8). The demon of scorpions and serpents Jesus identified as powerless towards his disciples are spirits (Luke 10:17-20). Satan is an "arch" dragon beast, all "principalities" are "arch-beginnings" spirits.

Angels who left their Beginning

*2 Peter 2:4, BLB: For if God did not spare **the angels having sinned**, but having cast them down to Tartarus, in chains of gloomy darkness, delivered them, being kept for judgment.*

*Jude 1:6, BLB: And **the angels not having kept their own domain**, but having abandoned the own dwelling, He keeps in eternal chains under darkness, unto the judgment of the great day.*

*Matthew 24:37-38, NASB: [37]"For the coming of the Son of Man will be just like the days of Noah. [38]"For as in those days before the flood they were eating and drinking, **marrying, and giving in marriage (lit., marryizing)**, until the day that Noah entered the ark,*

Another host of angels who sinned were angels who apparently cohabitated with human women. This occurred in the days of Noah and "also after that." In addition, Jesus also hinted that this type on sin related to angels would occur again. That is, Jessus spoke of two types of cohabitation in the days of Noah "marrying" and 'marryizing.'" In the days of Noah, not only were humans marrying (the acceptable form of marriage before God); but the sons of God were also illegally marrying the daughters of Adam, which Jesus called "marryizing." Both the Apostle Peter and Jude, the brother of James and our Lord Jesus, also both spoke of these angels that sinned. There sin was so severe that they were not allowed to continue as other Satan(s) are allowed to continue until Jesus eternal punishment is eventually meted out.

In Genesis chapter six, we learn that the "sons of God" choose wives from among the beautiful daughters of Adam. The result of the cohabitation is that "giants" were produced from this cohabitation. This form of marriage is what our Lord Jesus defined as "marryizing" that is the Greek word translated as "giving in marriage" is the Greek word "gamizontes." "Gamizontes" is a compound word of three Greek words: "gamos" (marriage), plus "iz" ("ize," to make like, conform like) and "ontes" (to exist, to be). Thus, some of the marriages in the days of Noah "conformed to" and "existed" like marriage, but it was not like God's original marriage in Genesis chapter two, man with women. This type of marrying related to the sons of God and Adam's daughters were called "marryizing," and it was sinful to do so.

In addition, "marryizing" also points to the sinful marriage of men with men, women with women, humanity with animals, and so forth. These "marryizing" are signs of the days Jesus spoke about that would happen again to also includes "marryizing" of humanity with angels, whether physical manifestation of these angels or spiritually in defiling dreams. Genesis chapter six, verses one through two, in conjunction with Jude chapter one, verses six through eight shows that the angels approached humans in their dreams and also in "instructing" those who they "tried" and deceived.

Jude 1:6-8a, NASB: *⁶And **angels** who did not keep their **own domain,** but abandoned their proper abode, He has kept in eternal bonds under darkness for the judgment of the great day, ⁷**just as Sodom and Gomorrah** and the cities around them, **since they in the same way as these indulged in gross immorality** and went after strange flesh ... ⁸**Yet in the same way** these men, also by dreaming, defile the flesh ....*

It is clear from the text above that the angels that sinned left their "own domain." The Greek reads that they "left their own beginning," and Jude did not stop there, he continues to say, their sin and punishment was "just as Sodom and Gomorrah" and pursued sex related to "'behind different' flesh." Jude continued by saying this type of sexuality started in their "dreams." So, what is considered "behind different flesh?" The appropriate flesh for sex is with a male and female pudenda. Sex with "different" or strange flesh is sex in the anus as Sodom and Gomorrah practiced and sex with angels as the men of Sodom and Gomorrah attempted to do with the angels who were sent to destroy Sodom and Gomorrah. Strange sex is also exemplified in the "sons of God" taking wives from among the daughters of Adam.

Genesis 19: 1-5, NASB: *¹Now **the two angels** came to Sodom in the evening as Lot was sitting in the gate of Sodom. When Lot saw them, he rose to meet them and bowed down with his face to the ground. ²And he said, "Now behold, my lords, please turn aside into your servant's house, and spend the night, and wash your feet; then you may rise early and go on your way." They said however, "No, but we shall spend the night in the square." ³Yet he urged them strongly, so they turned aside to him and entered his house; and he prepared a feast for them, and baked unleavened bread, and they ate. ⁴Before they lay down, **the men of the city, the men of Sodom, surrounded the house, both young and old, all the people from every quarter;** ⁵and they called to Lot and said to him, "Where are the men who came to you tonight? **Bring them out to us that we may have relations with them."***

Genesis 6:1-4, NASB: *1Now it came about, when men began to multiply on the face of the land, and **daughters** were born to them, 2that **the sons of God** saw that the daughters of men were **beautiful**; and they **took wives for themselves,** whomever they chose. ³Then the LORD said, "My Spirit shall not strive with man forever, because he also is flesh; nevertheless, his days shall be one hundred and twenty years." ⁴The **Nephilim** were on the earth in those days, and also afterward, **when the sons of God came in to the daughters of men,** and **they bore children to them.** Those were the mighty men who were of old, men of renown.*

The angels that sinned went after human flesh, which is strange flesh to them. The men of Sodom not only went after the strange flesh of "behind" flesh with both men and women, but they also pursued sexual relationships with angels. This is a grave sin; and God, after proper investigation of both happenings, determined that this type of angel sin must be dealt with swiftly; and the angels who sinned in this manner must be restricted from additional interaction with any of

God's creation both humans and angels. With that said, I will conclude this segment addressing some who don't believe the "sons of God" spoken of in Genesis chapter six are the "angels that sinned" spoken of by the Apostle Peter, or the "angels who left their own 'beginning'" spoken of by Jude. I will keep this succinct; and I recommend reading one of my other books, *Melchizedek*.

Sons of God Called Angels

The "sons of God" is witnessed in the scriptures to be the order of priests related to the Melchizedek order, also called "angels" with a **particular** eternal "house" related to humans designated "a house from heaven" and "eternal" (understood as such in Jude chapter one, verse six and second Corinthians chapter five, verses one through five; the only two places where the Greek word "oikētērion" is used).

In Genesis chapter six, verse four, the sons of God are given a paradoxical description. It is said of them, "those were the mighty men who were of old, men of renown;" which is literally translated as "mighty-men of eternity, mortals of the-name." How can they be "eternal" and yet considered "mortals?" Jude provided insight into a group of angels that sinned sexually like Sodom and Gomorrah.

They, "did not keep their beginning," but "left their own "house" ("oikētērion") similar to the eternal "house" ("oikētērion") humans will inherit through Jesus Christ. These "eternal mighty" were also called "mortals of **the-name.**" What name? The more excellent name "son" (Hebrews 1:1-2:9, Galatians 4:1-8, etcetera). I understand these "sons of God" to be of the Melchizedek order who are **"made similar to the Son of God."** All scholars agree that the sons of God in Genesis chapter six, were priests.

The high priest that existed then was Melchizedek and the priesthood under him; and priesthood is equated to "sons"

(Hebrews 5:5). This "Melchizedek," **who did not sin** as some of the other sons of God, **is indeed "made similar to the Son of God"** (Hebrew 7:3). Thus, Melchizedek would be considered a son of God, or a High Priest son among the priesthood of the sons of God (see Hebrews 5:5 where Jesus, the "Son" is equated to High Priest).

It follows that in order confirm that the "sons of God" in Genesis chapter six, who were also defined as "mortal of the name, mighty men of eternity" are known as "angels" the scripture of Truth must also witness to this; and Jesus said, the scriptures cannot be broken. The Word of God cannot be voided through men's opinion! That is, heaven and earth will pass away, however, the word of the Lord endures forever.

*Genesis 6:4, NASB: The Nephilim were on the earth in those days, and also afterward, when **the sons of God** came in to the daughters of men, and they bore children to them.*

*Hebrews 7:1; 3, NSASB: ¹For this Melchizedek, king of Salem, priest of the Most High God, who met Abraham .... ³Without father, without mother, without genealogy, having neither beginning of days nor end of life, **but made like the Son of God,** he remains a priest perpetually.*

*Daniel 3:24-25; 28: ²⁴Then Nebuchadnezzar the king was astonished, and rose up in haste, and spoke, and said unto his counselors, did not we cast **three men** bound into the midst of the fire? They answered and said unto the king, True, O king. ²⁵He answered and said, Lo, I see **four men** loose, walking in the middle of the fire, and they have no hurt; and the form of the fourth is **like the Son of God** .... ²⁸Then Nebuchadnezzar spoke, and said, Blessed be the God of Shadrach, Meshach, and Abednego, who hath sent **his angel,** and delivered his servants that trusted in him, and have changed the king's word, and yielded their bodies, that they might not serve nor worship any god, except their own God.*

In Daniel chapter three, we see that when the three Hebrew men stood up against Nebuchadnezzar's idol, related to the number of the beast, the number "because of man" — "666,"[9] they were cast into a furnace of fire. However, **"one like the Son of God"** was seen in the furnace of fire with them protecting them. This "one like the Son of God" is later called an "angel" in verse twenty-seven.

As "Melchizedek" was "made like the Son of God," so likewise there was one "like the Son of God," an "angel," who kept company with and delivered Hananiah, Mishael, and Azariah. These three brave men of faith received high priestly visits and deliverance in their trial. It follows that the "angels who sinned" can also be called "sons of God," because in Daniel chapter three verse twenty-five through verse twenty-eight, "angels" are equated to Melchizedek, "one like the Son of God." Thus, "sons of God" are also called "angels." In addition, there are some who say that because Jesus said, " spirits do not have flesh and bone as he had" (Luke 24:39); then the sons of God cannot be called angels, who are spirits.

However, they overlooked all the aspects of who can be defined as "spirit," and they understand not the power of God. In first Corinthians chapter fifteen, verses forty-two through forty-five, the Apostle Paul made it clear that Jesus' "resurrected" body, Jesus' "spiritual body" is a "'life-producing' **spirit.**" And therefore, Paul called Jesus' flesh and bone body, **"spirit."** Therefore, an understanding of Jesus' statement in Luke chapter twenty-four, verse thirty-nine and Paul's statement in first Corinthians fifteen, verse forty-five is

---

[9] The image of gold height was sixty (60) cubits, its 'opening' was six (6) cubits, and Nebuchadnezzar used six (6) types of musical instruments to coheres the people into serving and worshiping his image. It is also worthy to note that the number sixty (60) equals the gematria of the Hebrew word for "lie," seqer (שֶׁקֶר), 19, 21 and 20=60; and thus, "the lie" of idolatry, or image worship, is intertwined into the number of the beast (compare Revelation 14:9 – 13).

that there are different orders of "spirit," and some relate to the eternal body Jesus has and Jesus' saints will inherit.

Cherub who Sinned

Ezekiel 28:14-16, NASB: [14]*"You were the anointed* **cherub** *who covers, and I placed you there. You were on the holy mountain of God; you walked in the midst of the stones of fire.* [15]*"You were blameless in your ways from the day you were created until unrighteousness was found in you.* [16]*"By the abundance of your trade you were internally filled with violence,* **and you sinned;** *therefore, I have cast you as profane from the mountain of God. And I have destroyed you, O covering cherub, from the midst of the stones of fire."*

In Ezekiel we learn of Tyrus, the prince of Tyrus and the King of Tyrus. As we previously learned from Daniel chapter ten concerning the invisible prince and kings of Persia and reflected also in the natural with earthly kings and princes, so likewise the scriptures in Ezekiel chapter twenty-eight speaks both of a human prince of Tyrus and a spiritual **king of Tyrus, a cherub that also sinned in the garden of God.** In other words, the original serpent may have been the first beast of the field to sin from the beginning in the garden of Eden; however, the Word of God also documented another cherub that sinned in Eden (Ezekiel 28: 13-16). Like the original serpent, this cherub also began merchandising his holy things through his eventual pride related to the beauty he possessed. In other words, he began to "traffic" his "holy things" that were set apart for God's exclusive use by using his attractiveness to gain more than what God has already allotted to him. This is a classic example of idolatry, which is covetousness. This cherub was already "complete in beauty" (the beauty of worship to the living God, his drums were prepared in him); he was "full of wisdom" (all of the seven pillars of wisdom related to purity, peacefulness, tenderness, good persuaded, full of mercy and good fruit, no prejudice, and no hypocrisy); he also sealed the pattern (a pattern related to the Lord Jesus, which I will not develop in this book) — see Ezekiel 28:28:12-13, James 3:17.

However, through all this beauty, he desired more than he was allotted and began merchandising all of his beauty in his wisdom. Thus "he sinned" and became "violent," the opposite of "the wisdom from above." This same sin of violence of merchandising, through this cherub that sinned and the angel Satan who sins from the beginning, is continuing today in the world and in some entities related to the Church. This violence in marketing is seen in the marketing machine of mystery Babylon in the Book of Revelation chapter seventeen and Revelation chapter eighteen. This violence in marketing is seen in the merchandising of the saints by false prophets in second Peter chapter three. Jesus also exposed this violence in marketing that occurred in his days in the temple in Jerusalem in John chapter two, verses twelve through seventeen and Matthew chapter twenty-one, verses twelve through seventeen. This violence in marketing is seen in the covetousness of Satan's false prophets in second Corinthians chapters eleven and chapter twelve.

In conclusion, the sign of maturity or the sign that God with us is not gain or money that some have pursued through merchandising. The sign of maturity in God is not meeting some famous person or befriending some famous person, and thus having financial opportunity through merchandising. The sign of maturity is not being "over much" financially and "over much" numerically in people a person influences as some false apostles claim. The sign of maturity is not one's ability to merchandise God's people by selling millions of books or CDs or video recordings.

On the contrary, the sign of "maturity" or what the Bible calls "the mature man," those who reach "the measure of the stature of the fullness of Christ" is mature love. That is, love is the sign of maturity, not fame or money. The scriptures of Truth speaking of the maturity to come equated the mature person to mature love. The phrase "when that which is 'mature' is come" is equated to "becoming a man" of love, by putting away childish (immature) things (1 Corinthians 13:10-11; Ephesians 4:13, 1 Corinthians 13:1-8, 13, 1 John 4:12).

The Four Angels

Revelation 9:13-15, NASB: *¹³Then the sixth angel sounded, and I heard a voice from the four horns of the golden altar, which is before God, ¹⁴one saying to the sixth angel who had the trumpet, "Release **the four angels** who are **bound** at the great river Euphrates." ¹⁵And the four angels, who had been **prepared** for the hour and day and month and year, were released, so that they would **kill** a third of mankind.*

During the Sixth Trumpet, a voice came from the four horns of the golden altar directing the "Sixth Angel" who sounded the Sixth Trumpet giving the directive to "release the **four angels** who are **bound** at the great river Euphrates." The "Golden Altar" is the Altar of Incense; and incense is a symbol of the prayers of the saints (Revelation 5:8, Psalms 141); which means this command from the "horns of the golden 'sacrifice-place'" relates to prayer revealed in the Sixth Seal, the Seventh Trumpet, and the blood of Jesus. With that said, allow me to tell you of a personal experience before we discuss the four angels.

Around 1992 or 1993, I was frequenting the Lord, seeking understanding from the Book of Revelation. One of the many nights, I meditated all night on Revelation 9:13-20 repeatedly. As I continued to meditate deep into the morning hours, I saw a literal great light radiating from the Bible I was reading (meditating in). At around 7:00 am the Holy Spirit (the Spirit of wisdom and revelation) opened the scriptures of Revelation chapter nine, verses thirteen through twenty to me.

I was so excited about the wisdom the Lord gave me that morning I wanted to teach others immediately what the Lord revealed to me. However, he directed me to wait. When I did go to our Sunday morning meeting, one of the elders (Elder Gatewood) said to me that my countenance was very shiny. I knew then that the light I saw coming from the Bible was imparted to my body, spirit, and soul. That morning, after watching through the night, the Spirit of the Lord revealed to me the following.

Four Horns of the Golden Altar

*Revelation 9:13, NASB: Then the sixth angel sounded, and **I heard a voice from the four horns of the golden altar**, which is before God.*

The voice from the horns of the Golden Altar can speak to the Sixth Seal being fulfilled in this Sixth Trumpet related to the fulfillment of the request for vengeance of the souls who were slain for the Word of God and for the witness of Jesus they held (Revelation 6:9-11). The voice from the horns of the Golden Altar can also refer to the "prayers of all saints" revealed in the Seventh Seal in Revelation chapter eight, verses one through six being continued, because the Seventh Seal consists of all Seven Trumpets. More importantly, though, since the voice came from "the four horns of the Golden Altar," the voice can represent the voice of the blood of Jesus.

That is, in the Old Testament, the High Priest, once a year, on the Day of Atonement would sprinkle the blood of the sacrifices on the horns of the Golden Altar for atonement (Leviticus 16:18-19). In Hebrews chapter twelve, verse twenty-four, we learn that both Jesus' and Abel's blood "speaks" (Genesis 4:10). Therefore, the voice from the four horns of the Golden Altar can represent the voice of the blood of Jesus which has called for this judgment of the release of the four angels against those who have rejected Jesus' blood of God's covenant (Hebrews 10:29-30).

Four Angels Internally Prepared to Kill

Revelation 9:14-15, NASB: *14one saying to the sixth angel who had the trumpet, "Release **the four angels** who are **bound** at the great river **Euphrates**." 15And the four angels, who had been **prepared** for the hour and day and month and year, were released, so that they would **kill** a **third of mankind.***

These four angels had to be kept "bound" because God specifically designed them to "kill." That is, the Greek definition for the word "prepared" (hetoimazó) is properly translated as "internally prepared (Strongs #2090 with #2680). Therefore, these angels were "internally prepared" to kill, and they would kill constantly if they were not kept bound until the time of the sounding of the Sixth Trumpet. In addition, they were internally prepared to kill one-third (1/3) of humanity. This is a lot of people. Imagine what that would look like with the current world population of about nine billion. These four angels, unlike the previous locust-scorpions, did not come from the abyss. These were kept bound at the "great river Euphrates." Though this location of "Euphrates" may be literal to some, "Euphrates" has a prophetic and spiritual significance as we will see in a moment.

Four Angels Released

Revelation 9:14-16, NASB: *14one saying to the sixth angel who had the trumpet, "**Release the four angels** who are bound at the great river **Euphrates**." 15And the four angels, who had been prepared for **the hour and day and month and year,** were **released**, so that they would kill a third of mankind. 16The number of the armies of the horsemen was **two hundred million; I heard the number of them.***

The voice from the Golden Altar commanded to "release the four angels." Per Strong's Concordance the Greek word translated as "release" in the translation above or "loose" in another translation has a unique meaning. "Release" or "loose" means "to be reduced down to its constituent particles." This means the four (4) angels were "loosed" to multiply into two hundred million (200,000,000) horsemen, per oldest Greek text or 100,000,000 horsemen, per more recent Greek texts. Nonetheless, they multiplied from four angels into millions of beasts. The four angels were multiplied to their "constituent state." And for those who think this happening is singular, there are other examples in the Word of Truth.

In second Chronicles chapter eighteen, "a lying spirit" multiplied itself into the mouths of four hundred (400) false prophets. In Revelation sixteen, verses twelve through fourteen, in the Sixth Bowl of Wrath, we also see that Satan, the Beast and the False Prophet multiplied themselves by releasing frog spirits from their respective mouths. Also in Psalms sixty-eight, verse seventeen, the Hebrew text literally reads: "the chariots of God are tens of thousands, thousands **'changes,'** of the Lord."

In other words, some angels or spirits can change and multiply themselves into tens of thousands, thousands chariots. In the case of the four angels that were previously bound, they multiplied into two hundred million after they were "loosed" into their "constituent state." In addition, the fact that the four angels were released from the great river Euphrates also has spiritual significance. "Euphrates" is defined as, to break forth, to gush forth, or to rush forth, fruitfulness. That is, the angels shall be "loosed" into multiplication; they will "break forth" and "gush forth" as two hundred million horsemen.

The 200,000,000 Horsemen

Revelation 9:16-19: *¹⁶The number of the armies of the* **horsemen** *was two hundred million; I heard the number of them.* *¹⁷And this is how I saw in the vision the horses and those who sat on them: the riders had* **breastplates** *the* **color of fire** *and of* **hyacinth** *and of* **brimstone;** *and the heads of the horses are like* **the heads of lions;** *and out of their* **mouths** *proceed* **fire and smoke and brimstone.** *¹⁸A third of mankind was killed by these three plagues, by the fire and the smoke and the brimstone which proceeded out of their mouths.* *¹⁹For the power of the horses is in* **their mouths and in their tails;** *for their tails are like serpents and have heads, and with them they do harm.*

The four angels, now released and multiplied into two hundred million (200,000,000) horsemen, also manifested symbolically in their armor the plagues they would release on one-third of mankind. (These plagues can be released only "for an hour," or "for a day," or "for a month," or "for a year" at God's choosing.) The breastplates were "fiery shiny," "hyacinth" (dark purple or dark blue), and "brimstone like."

That is, "the heads of the horses," the horses the now multiplied angelic beings rode, "are like the heads of lions;" and their "tails are like serpents having heads" and "out of their mouths" (both the mouth of the lions heads and the mouth of the serpents heads) "proceed **fire** and **smoke** and **brimstone.**" Thus, the "fiery" color in their breastplates is associated with the judgment of "fire." The "hyacinth" of their breastplates is associated with the dark colored "smoke." The brimstone-like portion of the breastplates is associated with the judgment by lightning strike.

Fire, Smoke, Brimstone

The plague by fire means just that. These lion headed and snake tailed horses will release fire from their mouths that will kill. And since the Greek word for fire is also associated with the Greek word for "fever," some will also die through plagues that cause fever. The plague by hyacinth smoke, if one looks at hyacinth relative to its common color of dark purple or dark blue, the smoke then being a dark purple-blue color, kills through inhalation (compare Revelation 9:2). If hyacinth is looked at through ancient Greek cultural mythology, then hyacinth may relate to judgment against accepted commonality of same sexuality. With regards to brimstone, the Greek word for brimstone is "theion" — "a place struck by lightning" and gives off a smell, or God fire. Therefore, out of the horses with lion heads, and the heads of horses' serpent tails, lightning, and the smell of being struck by lightning will also kill those who are practicing the things outlined in Revelation chapter nine, verses twenty and twenty-one.

People Repented Not

Revelation 9:20-21, NASB: *[20]The rest of mankind, who were not killed by these plagues, did not repent of the works of their hands, so as not to worship demons, and the idols of gold and of silver and of brass and of stone and of wood, which can neither see nor hear nor walk; [21]and they did not repent of their murders nor of their sorceries nor of their immorality nor of their thefts.*

The conclusion of these plagues reveals the reason the plagues of the four angels were released in the first place; and the list is telling; yet to most of humanity some of these practices are accepted as norm. These plagues were released for the practices of worship of demons, worship of idols of gold and of silver and of brass and of stone and of wood, which can neither see nor hear nor walk. These plagues were also released because of murders, the practice of sorceries, sexual immorality, and thefts. These practices must have gotten so bad on the earth, as mankind rejected the atoning blood of Jesus, that the time came when the Sixth Angel sounded the Sixth Trumpet to release these plagues. Yet there was a very sad conclusion, the remaining living who did not die from these plagues, probably had a scientific explanation for the vast death toll and "did not repent." Here are the words of our Lord Jesus when he began his public ministry: "Now after John had been taken into custody, **Jesus** came into Galilee, **preaching the gospel of God,** and saying, "The time is fulfilled, and the kingdom of God is at hand; **repent and believe in the gospel"** (Mark 1:14-15).

Myriads of Angels

Hebrews 12:22, NASB: But **you have come** *to Mount Zion and to the city of the living God, the heavenly Jerusalem, and to* **myriads of angels.**

Matthew 26:53: "Or do you think that I cannot appeal to My Father, and He will at once put at My disposal more than **twelve legions of angels."**

Our Lord Jesus stated in Matthew chapter twenty-six, verse fifty-three that he could appeal to his heavenly Father to dispatch twelve legions of angels to defend him from those who were about to unjustly seize him to be crucified. However, Jesus did not use this authority, because if he did, he could not fulfill the scripture that he is to be crucified. Yet, the access to these myriad of angels is still true. The writer of the Book of Hebrews reiterated a similar principle. The believers in Christ "have come," not will come, but "have come to... myriads of angels." Thus, in this chapter, my intent is to review some of these angels, which is by no means exhaustive in scope.

Cherubs or Cherubim

Genesis 3:24, NASB: So He drove the man out; and at the east of the garden of Eden He stationed the **cherubim** *and the flaming sword which turned every direction to guard the way to the tree of life.*

God's angels are gifted with various powers or weapons of power. In Genesis chapter three, we see the first mention of "a flaming sword" and "cherubs" or "cherubim." Both of these entities God sent as "guards" of the way to the tree of life. Thus, "cherubs" are guardians God established. Also, the one of the definitions for "cherubs" or "cherubim" is "as-multitude." Thus, as we learned in the chapter on "The Four Angels," cherubim can multiply or expand themselves into a multitude of beings. The Hebrew words for cherub are as

91

follows: [(כרוב) krub], [(כרב) krb], and the plural forms for cherubs are krubim (כרובים) or krbim (כרבים). "Krubim" with the "u" (Hebrew vav) in its spelling is found in first Kings chapter six, verse twenty-three (1 Kings 6:23); and "krbim" without the "u" in its spelling is found in first Kings chapter six verse twenty-five, verse twenty-seven, first Chronicle chapter twenty-eight, verse eighteen and Exodus Chapter twenty-five, verse eighteen (1 Kings 6:25; 6:27, 1 Chronicle 28:18 and Exodus 25:18).

The Holy Spirit providing both forms of spelling for cherubs is one of the keys to unlocking this mystery relating to the definition of "krb" (cherub). In the Book of Hebrews chapter seven, the mystery of Melchizedek is initially interpreted to us through the definition and translation of Melchizedek's name and the definition and translation of the city he ruled; "Melchizedek … **first being by interpretation (or lit., translation)** King of righteousness, and after that also King of Salem, which is King of peace" (Hebrews 7:1-2).

That is, **cherub, ("krb"),** the singular form of **cherubim** ("krbim") is translated as **"according unto the multitude"** (see Psalm 106:45, Psalm 51:1). "Krb" is made up of the prefix "kaph" (כ) and the word "rb"(רב). In the Hebrew language when "kaph" (כ) is used as a prefix to a word, "kaph" (כ) means "as" which means "to use something in comparison" (Oxford). "Rb" by definition means **multitude,** vast, great, abundance, **myriad,** and so on. Hence, the translation of "krb" in the Psalms referenced above is also a valid translation of "cherub." That is, "cherubs" also represents God's "comparison" ("as") to God's "multitude" of angels or God's "myriad" of angels.

Also, in Ezekiel chapter eleven, the "living creatures" described in Ezekiel chapter one are called "cherubs." The cherubs are described as magnificent beings with four wings, four faces, large bisecting wheels, feet like a calf, eyes all over their bodies, their wings gives the sound of speech, and so forth. They are beings that transport the Lord Jesus in the Spirit (Ezekiel 1:26-28); and they move as fast as lightning on right angels (Ezekiel 1:12-13). Thus, be sure, they are nothing to play with; they are powerful "guardians" that see every which way and are quick as lightning on their feet.

Ezekiel 1:5-8, NASB: *⁵And within it there were figures resembling* **four living beings**. *And this was their appearance: they had human form.* *⁶Each of them had* **four faces and four wings**. *⁷Their legs were straight and their feet were like a calf's hoof, and they sparkled like polished bronze.* *⁸Under their wings on their four sides were human hands. As for the faces and wings of the four of them.*

Ezekiel 10:5, NASB: Then the **cherubim** *rose up.* **They are the living beings** *that I saw by the river Chebar.*

With that said, **cherub**s in Ezekiel chapter one coupled with the chariot cherubs Solomon made and the cherubs on the Ark of the Covenant that Moses made are **also representative of the corporate matured body of Christ**, "as (God's) multitudes" of mature believer, which is too lengthy to develop in this book.[10] Finally, it is also worthy to note that since we now understand that the "cherubim" are called "living creatures" or "living beings;" let us look at this understanding relative to the second set of "beasts" the Lord created in Genesis chapter two, verse nineteen, of which the original serpent is identified as one of the second sets of "beasts."

The phrase "living creatures" is translated as "beasts" of the field in Genesis chapter two and chapter three. Therefore, the "living beings" or "beasts" of the field, in Genesis chapter three, verse one, can be understood to be cherubs or seraphs. These "beast of the field" are different from the first set of

---

[10] You may refer to my book *Ezekiel, the House-the City, the Land, Interpreting the Patters under "cherubs" for further development.*

"beasts of the earth" created in Genesis chapter one verses twenty-four and twenty-five, and some of the "beasts of the earth" were described as cattle ("dumb beasts") and creeping things. The "beasts of the field," however, can speak (Genesis 3:1-5, Isaiah 6:1-4, Revelation 4:8).

*Ezekiel 1:5-8, NASB: ⁵And within it there were figures resembling four **living beings**. And this was their appearance: they had human form. ⁶**Each of them had four faces** and four wings.*

*Genesis 3:1a, NKJV: Now the **serpent** was more cunning than any **beast (or living creatures)** of the field which the Lord God had made ....*

*Revelation 12:9a; 14: ⁹ᵃAnd the **great dragon** was cast out, that **old (lit., original) serpent**, called the **Devil**, and **Satan** .... ¹⁴And to the woman were given two wings of a great eagle, that she might fly into the wilderness, into her place, where she is nourished for a time, and times, and half a time, from the **face of the serpent**.*

Here is the biblical logic that shows that the original serpent was probably a cherub with at least four wings (one of the characteristics of cherubs, or he may have six wings, one of the characteristics of seraphs). The cherubs, in Ezekiel chapter one, all have four faces per head: the face lion, the face of an ox, the face of a man, the face of an eagle. In Revelation chapter twelve, we see that the original serpent apparently has four faces per head, dragon, serpent, Satan, Devil. That is, since the scripture says there is a "face of the serpent," there is also a "face" of the great dragon. There is a face of Satan. There is a face of the Devil. In addition, the cherubs described in Ezekiel chapters one and ten all have four wings.

Thus, the "beasts of the field" can be understood as "'living creatures' of the field," or cherubs, of which the original serpent with his four faces was a part of. It follows that those "beasts of the field" may be an order of cherubs who were originally created to also be guards **for** the living God.

However, some did not stand in the Truth and sinned. And note, according to Ezekiel chapter twenty-eight, there was another cherub who also sinned in the garden of God, the third heaven.

Seraphs or Seraphim

Isaiah 6:1-3, NASB: ¹*In the year of King Uzziah's death I saw the Lord sitting on a throne, lofty and exalted, with the train of His robe filling the temple.* ²***Seraphim** were standing above Him, each having **six wings:** with two each covered his face, and with two each covered his feet, and with two each flew.* ³*And one called out to another and said, "Holy, Holy, Holy, is the LORD of armies. The whole earth is full of His glory."*

In Isaiah chapter six, we learn of another group of "living beings" or angels called "Seraphs" or "Seraphim." These are a little different from cherubs in that they are "burning-ones" who can set on fire, or they are fiery (See Strong's #8313, 8314). They also have six wings, in lieu of four wings; and are authorized to use the live coals off of the altar to purge sins (Isaiah 6:5-7). More importantly, they constantly worship the Lord saying, "holy, holy, holy, is the Lord of host, the whole earth is full of his glory."

These seraphs are also understood to be the "living creatures" in Revelation chapter four, where they are also described with their "six wings" having the individual heads that match those of the cherubs in Ezekiel chapter one. Except the seraphim do not appear to have four faces each for each head. In Revelation chapter four, the apparent seraphs each were described as a lion, an ox, a man-faced being, and a flying eagle, having eyes all over their bodies and six wings each.

If one also include the description of them in Isaiah chapter six, these seraph have the ability to transform into "burning ones;" and maybe in their burning forms, they still maintain a burning form of a man faced being, burning form of an ox, burning form of a flying eagle and a burning form of a lion. In addition, both descriptions of these living beings, highlight their worshiping of the Lord's holiness, day, and night. In Revelation chapter four, they worship saying, **"holy, holy, holy** is the Lord God Almighty, he who was, who is and who is to come."** In Isaiah chapter six, they worship the Lord saying, **"holy, holy, holy**, is the Lord of host, the who earth is filled with his glory."

Revelation 4:6-8, NASB: ⁶*and before the throne there was something like a sea of glass, like crystal; and in the center and around the throne,* ***four living creatures*** *full of eyes in front and behind.* ⁷*The first living creature was like a lion, the second creature like a calf, the third creature had a face like that of a man, and the fourth creature was like a flying eagle.* ⁸*And the four living creatures,* ***each one of them having six wings,*** *are full of eyes around and within; and* ***day and night they do not cease*** *to say,* ***"HOLY, HOLY, HOLY IS THE LORD GOD, THE ALMIGHTY,*** *who was and who is and who is to come."*

Isaiah 6:1-3, NASB: ¹*In the year of King Uzziah's death I saw the Lord sitting on a throne, lofty and exalted, with the train of His robe filling the temple.* ²*Seraphim were standing above Him, each having* ***six wings:*** *with two each covered his face, and with two each covered his feet, and with two each flew.* ³*And one called out to another and said,* ***"Holy, Holy, Holy, is the LORD of armies. The whole earth is full of His glory."***

Thus, the Seraphs are **burning ministering spirits** who minister to the Lord's holiness in worship. In Hebrews chapter one, verse seven it is written, "And of the angels He says: "Who makes His angels spirits and His ministers a **flame of fire.**" The Book of Hebrews also says, "let all the angels of God **worship him**" (Hebrews 1:6). The seraphs can also use the burning coals from the altar to minister purification, in the Spirit, from iniquity from those who repent before the Lord, as exemplified with the Prophet Isaiah (Isaiah 6:5-8).

They also are involved in the distribution of the Seven Bowls of Wrath in Revelation chapter fifteen; and they are also involved in the sending forth of the events of the Seven Seals the Lamb of God loosed from the scroll in Revelation chapter six. In Revelation chapter eight, verse thirteen, the "eagle flying" in midheaven may be representative of one of the seraphs that is described as a "flying eagle." Therefore, the seraphs are also an integral part of announcing the "woes" of the last three trumpets (the fifth, the sixth and seventh trumpets). That is, these seraphs are not static beings in the Spirit. They are dynamic creatures also involved in the workings of the living God, especially with regards to purging of sin, as in Isaiah's case, or by discipline the Lord meets out to those who sin against God, exemplified in the days of Moses in Numbers chapter twenty-one.

Seraphim Serpents

*Numbers 21:6: And the LORD sent **fiery serpents (or seraphs serpents)** among the people, and they bit the people; and **much (vast)** people of Israel died.*

In the Book of Numbers "seraphs" or "seraphim" are also associated with "serpents." These "seraphim serpents" were sent against the sons of Israel for speaking against God and Moses. If we understand these seraphim serpents in light of Isaiah chapter six, then these seraphim serpents can be understood as serpents from the invisible that God used to address the sin of the people who spoke against God and Moses. To show that these seraphim serpents could be of heavenly origin, Jesus liken himself to the "serpent of brass" God commanded Moses to fabricate a "seraph" made of brass in order to cause those who were "bitten" by the seraphim serpents to live, once they look upon the seraph Moses was to make.

*Numbers 21:6-9: ⁶And the LORD sent **fiery serpents (or seraphs serpents)** among the people, and they **bit** the people; and much people of Israel died. ⁷Therefore, the people came to Moses, and said, we have sinned, for we have spoken against the LORD, and against you; pray unto the LORD, that he take away the serpents from us. And Moses prayed for the people. ⁸And the LORD said unto Moses, Make you a **fiery serpent (lit., seraph),** and set it upon a pole: and it shall come to pass, that every one that is bitten, when he looks upon it, shall live. ⁹And Moses made a **serpent of brass,** and put it upon a pole, and it came to pass, that if a serpent had bitten any man, **when he beheld the serpent of brass, he lived.***

*John 3:14-15: ¹⁴And as Moses lifted up the **serpent** in the wilderness, even so must the Son of man be lifted up: ¹⁵That whosoever believeth in him should not perish but have eternal life.*

Jesus likened himself to the "serpent" Moses lifted up in the wilderness; and this narrative concerning the "brass serpent" Moses made is filled with truth that may apply to the seraphim. That is, the Lord directed Moses to make a "seraph." Moses then made a "serpent of brass," called of God a "seraph." Thus, the "seraphs serpents" that bit the people were indeed "serpents." In addition, our Lord Jesus was also alluding that there are many spiritually dead who have been bitten by serpents; and if they look to Jesus, they will be forgiven their sins and not perish.

Jesus became a "serpent;" that is, Jesus was "**made sin** who knew no sin that we might be made the righteousness of God in him" (2 Corinthians 5:21). Yes, when Jesus was "lifted up" on the cross he became the "serpent of brass" that gave life to those who look to him. It is also worthy to note that the Hebrew word for **"brass"** consists of the Hebrew word for "serpent" with the letter "tav" (a symbol of the cross, covenant, etcetera) at the end of the word. Thus, "brass" represents a "serpent-crucified" or a "crucified-serpent."

Jesus was made sin on the cross, he became the "serpent-crucified" in order for us to live! With all that said, the "seraphim serpents" in Numbers chapter twenty-one coupled with Isaiah, chapter six, verse two, provides another vantage point of seraphim. That is, not only can seraphim be understood as being in the form of a lion with six wings, a calf with six wings, a man faced being with six wings, and a flying eagle with six wings; they can be in the form of serpents; and they are apparently used for discipline related to speaking against God and those whom God has placed as leaders!

Jesus' Elect Angels

*1 Timothy 5:21, NKJV: I charge you before God and the Lord Jesus Christ and the **elect angels** that you observe these things without prejudice, doing nothing with partiality.*

Per the Apostle Paul, there are "elect angels" who "witness" our behavior with respect to honoring Church elders financially and with respect to not accepting singular false accusations against church elders. To show Timothy the seriousness of his request to honor elders, and not accepting singular accusations, Paul made it clear that God, the Lord Jesus Christ, and the elect angels are called upon to observe Timothy's behavior. There are principles in this statement concerning the elect angels that are worthy to be reviewed. First, let us look at the entire context of Paul's statement.

*1 Timothy 5:17-21, NKJV: [17]Let the elders who rule well be counted worthy of **double honor**, especially **those who labor in the word and doctrine**. [18]For the Scripture says, "You shall not muzzle an ox while it treads out the grain," and, "The laborer is worthy of his wages." [19]**Do not receive an accusation against an elder except from two or three witnesses.** [20]Those who are sinning rebuke in the presence of all, that the rest also may fear. [21]I charge you before **God and the Lord Jesus Christ** and the **elect angels** that you observe these things without prejudice, doing nothing with partiality.*

First, these "elect angels" are apparently angels who were chosen due to their intense "double honor" for the eternal God and the Lord Jesus Christ. The elect angels did not accept the "accusations" of the angel Satan against Jesus, the Truth, and God's Truth of his preordained plans for mankind. In other words, the elect angels "stood" in the "Truth" of God and the Truth concerning Jesus, even though the original serpent, Satan, and his angels brought false "accusation" to angels concerning the elder eternal Father and the elder Ancient of Days, Jesus. The elect angels maintained their honor towards the living God and the Lord Jesus with their loyalty and did not accept satanic accusations in any form.

Yes, one of Satan's sins from the beginning is that he did "not stand in the Truth" (John 4:44) as he falsely accused the heavenly Father and the Son, our Lord Jesus. However, the elect angels rejected Satan's notion, settled the "argument," and remained honorable to the living God and our Lord Jesus. This can be understood as we look at the definition of the word "elect" in the context of the first Timothy chapter five, verses seventeen through twenty-one cited earlier. That is, a person will see that God also chose the elect angels bringing an end to any accusatory argument.

"Eklektós" (elect) means "to select, choose," properly, selected (chosen from, out of), especially as a deeply personal choice. As one looks at the root words for "elect" it will also be seen that it means "to select (choose) out of, by a highly **deliberate** choice (i.e., real heart-preference) with a definite outcome." Finally, the root "lego" means to **bring an argument to rest.**

Thus, in context of Paul admonition to Timothy, citing God, the Lord Jesus, and the elect angels, relative to proper honor of elders and the refusal of singular false accusations against elders, there must have been an "argument," not just when Paul penned this truth some two thousand years ago; but

Paul's writing gives us a glimpse of why these angels were considered "elected" in the first place from the beginning. There was apparently an "argument" or arguments among the angels, instigated by the accusations of Satan (compare Jude 1:9).

As Jesus said, in the beginning, and also presently, Satan did not "stand in the Truth" that God established. In addition, Satan, the accuser of the brothers and sisters, also spued out accusations against God and the Lord Jesus in opposition to the Truth. And as we learned earlier Satan, then exalted himself above all that is called God or worshiped (God the Father, God the Son, God the Spirit). And since Satan is to be judged in the "eternal fire," he must have also "blasphemed" the "eternal Spirit," which is the "eternal sin" (Mark 3:28-30).

However, the "elect angels" did not accept those accusations from Satan. They did not dishonor the elder eternal God. They did not dishonor the Son, Jesus; and they did not tamper with Adam and Eve, as Satan did and was cursed of God. Thus, God "laid the argument to rest" and "elected" the angels who continued to honor him. God made "a deep personal" and "highly deliberate" choice with regards to the elect angels. God chose them for their honorable stand in the Truth of God. Hence, Paul encouraged his spiritual son Timothy to honor the elders and not receive any accusation against an elder without two or three witnesses. Honor the elders with double pay because it is laborious to work in the Word of God and to teach. This truth needs to be taught to the believer of today of how to properly honor the elders who "rule well," and not to follow the accuser's "modus operandi."

Jesus' Holy Angels

*Mark 8:38, NASB: "For whoever is **ashamed of Me** and My words in this **adulterous and sinful generation**, the Son of Man will also be ashamed of him when He comes in the glory of His Father with **the holy angels.**"*

*Revelation 14:9-10, NASB: [9]Then another angel, a third one, followed them, saying with a loud voice, "If anyone worships the beast and his image, and receives a mark on his forehead or on his hand, [10]he also will drink of the wine of the anger of God, having been mixed undiluted in the cup of His wrath; and he will be tormented in fire and brimstone before the **holy angels** and before the Lamb.*

"Holy angels" (plural) are translated as such in the New Testament twice and once in the singular. Holy angels can also be found in the Book of Daniel, chapters four and eight. "Holiness" is usually contrasted against unholiness. In the context of Mark chapter eight, verse thirty-eight, Jesus and his holy angels are contrasted against those who are ashamed of him related to unholy living of adultery and sin. Thus, these holy angels are also witnesses of the Lord Jesus with respect to holy living.

Also, in context of Revelation chapter fourteen, verses nine and ten, the holy angels with the Lamb, will witness the torment of those who participate in the unholy worship of the beast and those who receive the unholy mark of the beast. That is, humanity who reject the sacrifices of Jesus, the Lamb of God, as an "unholy thing"[11] will be tormented and publicly witnessed by the holy angels. With that said, let us now take a look at Acts chapter ten, verse twenty-two, where a holy angel was identified.

---

[11] Hebrews 10:29-30

*Acts 10:22; 34-36; 38 NASB: They said, "Cornelius, a centurion, a righteous and God-fearing man well-spoken of by the entire nation of the Jews, was divinely directed by a **holy angel** to send for **you (Apostle Peter)**to come to his house and hear a **message from you** .... ³⁴Opening his mouth, Peter said: "I most certainly understand now that God is not one to show partiality, ³⁵but in every nation the man who fears Him and does what is right is welcome to Him. ³⁶"The word which He sent to the sons of Israel, **preaching peace through Jesus Christ (He is Lord of all)** ....³⁸"You know of Jesus of Nazareth**, how God anointed Him with the Holy Spirit and with power, and how He went about doing good and healing all who were oppressed by the devil, for God was with Him.'*

Cornelius, while on a fast, received "an oracle" or an appraisal from a holy angel for him to seek out Apostle Peter for the words of Jesus' salvation (Acts 10:34-48). The holy angel did not give a revised doctrine concerning Jesus Christ as some angels may have done according to Galatians, chapter one, or a revision of pure religion some religions have claimed to receive from angels that currently govern whole nations or certain ethnics.

The holy angel directed Cornelius to seek out the Apostle Peter who preached Jesus to Cornelius. Thus, if any angel preaches any other gospel and any other Jesus and offer any other spirit, other than the Holy Spirit and the gospel of Jesus Christ, the gospel the Apostles of the Lamb preached, and the gospel the Apostles of Christ as Paul, Silas and Timothy preached, they are unholy angels. They are the angels of Satan(s) transforming themselves as angels of light.

*2 Corinthians 11:4; 13-15, NKJV: ⁴For if he who comes preaches **another Jesus** whom we have not preached, or if you receive a different spirit which you have **not** received, or a different gospel which you have not accepted — you may well put up with it! .... ¹³For such **are false apostles,** deceitful workers, transforming themselves into apostles of Christ. ¹⁴And no wonder! For **Satan himself transforms himself into an angel of light**. ¹⁵Therefore*

103

it is no great thing if his ministers also transform themselves into ministers of righteousness, whose end will be according to their works.

Galatians 1:8-9: *⁸But even if we, or **an angel from heaven, preach any other gospel** to you than what we have preached to you, **let him be accursed.** ⁹As we have said before, so now I say again, if anyone preaches any other gospel to you than what you have received, let him be accursed.*

The verses above are clear, Satan, his angels, his false apostle, his false ministers are the only ones who preach any other gospel, other than the gospel of Truth. **The holy angels of God will only lead people to true apostles, true prophets, true ministers of the gospel of Jesus Christ to hear the gospel of Truth.** The gospel of Truth is never race based, nationality based, formal education based, or financially based. For example, God does want his people to prosper; however, our prosperity is not to be construed to represent godliness or richness toward God (1 Timothy 6:3-5, Luke 12:21). This will be discussed further when "religion of angels" are exposed. With that said, the Book of Daniel also revealed "holy" angels also called "watchers" or also called "sentinels" in the Septuagint (LXX).

Daniel 4:13-14; 23, NKJV: *¹³"I saw in the visions of my head while on my bed, and there **was a watcher, a holy one,** coming down from heaven. ¹⁴He cried aloud and said thus: 'Chop down the tree and cut off its branches ... 23"And inasmuch as the king saw a **watcher, a holy one,** coming down from heaven and saying, 'Chop down the tree and destroy it, but leave its stump and roots in the earth, bound with a band of iron and bronze in the tender grass of the field; let it be wet with the dew of heaven, and let him graze with the beasts of the field, till **seven times** pass over him.'"*

*Daniel 8:13, NKJV: Then I heard **a holy one** speaking; and **another holy one** said to **'Palmoni'** who was speaking, "How long will the vision be, concerning the daily sacrifices and the transgression of desolation, the giving of both the sanctuary and the host to be trampled underfoot?"*

Again, without getting into the details of Daniel chapter four, except to say that in a dream God revealed to Nebuchadnezzar that he would be humbled if he continued in his pride. This humbling would be through the words of a holy one and a watcher. Thus, some of God's holy angels, called "holy ones" and "watchers" are "sentinels" who watch over kings and kingdoms. God uses these holy angels or watchers to abase these earthly kings. In Nebuchadnezzar's case he was humbled for approximately seven months.

In other words, there is a standard of holiness in the holy angels that measures abuses related to pride, the treatment of the poor, etcetera; and God had granted the holy angels and watchers this discretion to judge unholiness. For it is said in Daniel chapter four, verse seventeen, concerning the humbling of king Nebuchadnezzar, "this **decision is by the decree of the watchers,** and **the sentence by the word of the holy ones,** in order that the living may know that the Most High rules in the kingdom of men, gives it to whomever He will, and sets over it the lowest of men."

It is worthy to also highlight that when the holy angel appeared to Cornelius, the centurion, his' "prayers" and "alms giving" were acknowledged, which is something king Nebuchadnezzar did not practice with regards to showing mercy to the poor (Daniel 4:27). Hence, in Cornelius's case, he received the blessings of salvation through the direction of the holy angel and through the preaching of Jesus Christ by the Apostle Peter. However, Nebuchadnezzar, received another decision by the holy angels, humiliation.

Angels of Jesus' Power

2 Thessalonians 1:6-7, NASB: *[6]For after all it is only just for God to repay with affliction those who afflict you, [7]and to give relief to you who are afflicted and to us as well when **the Lord Jesus** will be revealed from heaven with **His mighty angels (lit., angels of his power) in flaming fire.***

*Joshua 5:14, LXX: "but he said to him, I am **"archsoldier"** (of the) power (of the) Lord."*

Among Jesus' holy angels, Jesus' elect angels are also angels of Jesus' power. That is, there are angels who flow in power; and these power angels are also used to judge unbelievers and angels who do not stand in the Truth. We learned in a previous chapter about the "archsoldier" who is the "prince" of the power of the Lord. Thus, there will be war when Jesus returns between the unbeliever who worship the dragon and the beast, those who reject the gospel of our Lord Jesus Christ, those who do not know God; and these unbelievers will experience the angels of Jesus' power in a strong way.

2 Thessalonians 1:6-7, NASB: *[6]For after all it is only just for God to repay with affliction those who afflict you, [7]and to give relief to you who are afflicted and to us as well when **the Lord Jesus** will be revealed from heaven with **His mighty angels (lit., angels of his power) in flaming fire,** [8]dealing out retribution to those **who do not know God** and to those who **do not obey** the gospel of our Lord Jesus. [9]These will pay the penalty of **eternal destruction**, away from the presence of the Lord and from the glory of **His power**, [10]when He comes to be glorified in His saints on that day ....*

Revelation 19:11-16, NASB: *[11]And I saw heaven opened, and behold, a white horse, and He who sat on it is called Faithful and True, **and in righteousness He judges and wages war.** [12]His eyes are a flame of fire, and on His head are many diadems; and He has a name written on Him which no one knows except Himself. [13]He is clothed with a robe dipped in blood, and **His name is called The***

Word of God. ¹⁴And the armies which are in heaven, clothed in fine linen, white and clean, were following Him on white horses. 15From His mouth comes a sharp sword, so that with it He may strike down the nations, and He will rule them with a rod of iron; and He treads the wine press of the fierce wrath of God, the Almighty. *16And on His robe and on His thigh He has a name written, "KING OF KINGS, AND LORD OF LORDS."*

Our Angels

*Matthew 18:10, NASB: 10"See that you do not despise one of these little ones, for I say to you that **their angels** in heaven **continually see the face of My Father** who is in heaven.*

*Acts 12:13-15, NASB: 13When he knocked at the door of the gate, a slave woman named Rhoda came to answer. **14When she recognized Peter's voice,** because of her joy she did not open the gate, but ran in and announced that Peter was standing in front of the gate. 15They said to her, "You are out of your mind!" But she kept insisting that it was so. **They said, "It is his angel."***

Jesus revealed that there are angels that are assigned to his "little ones," his disciples who believe that Jesus is the Christ, the Son of the living God. Jesus called the angels of those who believe in him "their angels." Thus, among the myriads of angels, some of them are assigned to each believer. In our case, "our angels" take their cue from the "face" our heavenly Father as to how to respond to their respective assignment. Jesus defined one of the qualifications for our angel's response to us, relates to us being "despised." This was exemplified with Apostle Peter in Acts chapter twelve. Herod recently despised and slew Apostle James, the brother of the beloved Apostle John. He then proceeded to imprison Peter to also slay him. However, the saints prayed for Peter. As they agreed in prayer for Peter as a symphony, the Lord assigned an angel to free Peter supernaturally.

However, after Peter was freed by the hand of the angel, Peter went to the saints, in secret, to tell them of the aid the angel of the Lord provided in his release. Upon arriving at the gate of the home, the saints were still praying for Peter, not knowing the Lord Jesus heard their prayer and sent an angel to free Peter. When the young lady told the other saints that Peter was at the gate, they rejected her as being "mad." This should be a lesson to us. They were praying for Peter to be released. The Lord heard their prayer and sent his angel and released Peter. Yet when they were told that Peter escaped and was at their gate they thought the young lady was mad. However, she kept being persistent with them that she indeed heard Peter's voice at the gate asking for entrance; then they finally made another statement to the young lady, they said, **"it is his angel."** This statement also speaks volume. In the believers mind of those days, the voice of "their angels" sounds like the person the angel is assigned to minister to. In addition, "their angels" also looked like them because they were convinced that it could not be Peter knocking, but "his angel" which sounded and looked like Peter. This understanding is true. I experienced something similar, where my angel appears to look like me.

My Angel

In 1993, during a season of intense testing, the Lord asked me to close my business to seek Him in prayer, study and fasting. What I thought was to be a short time turned out to be about three to four years of Jesus molding me through testing and trials. I came to the end of myself during this time of testing and was overly anxious about provision for my family on a particular day that no provision came through to us in a timely manner. The following morning, as I was praying to God for direction with regards to provisions for us, I saw in a vision my angel standing next to me by the door. He was dressed in jeans, boots, and a belt with a significant belt buckle. He was standing and leaning against the wall by the door. As I turned to look at him closer, he vanished. The angel looked like me. He stood like I would. A few seconds thereafter, in a clear voice, the Lord or the angel of the Lord, spoke to me that morning concerning my provision.

He told me to take one of my carpentry power tools I had left after I closed the business in obedience to the Lord; and go to the pawn shop. He also said to me specifically, when I get to the door of the shop a man will be there waiting for me and will turn to me immediately and ask me "How much do you need?" It happened just as the voice of the Lord said. As my feet crossed the threshold of the pawn shop, a gentleman turned to me in a very courteous manner and asked me, "How much do you need?" It was delightful to me to see how specific the Lord was in his knowing the man's response, and the fact that the Lord manifested to me that "my angel" is present and will respond according to the direction of my heavenly Father. I asked the man for what the carpenter's saw was worth and received that amount.

Matthew 18:10, NASB: [10]*"See that you do not despise one of these little ones, for I say to you that **their angels** in heaven **continually see the face of My Father** who is in heaven.*

Acts 12:13-15, NASB: [13]*When he knocked at the door of the gate, a slave woman named Rhoda came to answer.* [14]***When she recognized Peter's voice,** because of her joy she did not open the gate, but ran in and announced that Peter was standing in front of the gate.* [15]*They said to her, "You are out of your mind!" But she kept insisting that it was so. **They said, "It is his angel."***

Religion of Angels

Colossians 2:18-19: [18]*Take care that no one keeps defrauding you of your prize by delighting in humility and the* **worship of the angels,** *taking his stand on visions he has seen, inflated without cause by his fleshly mind,* [19]*and* **not holding firmly to the head,** *from whom the entire body, being supplied and held together by the joints and ligaments, grows with a growth which is from God.*

The phrase "worship of the angels" is better translated as "religion of angels." The Greek word "thréskeia" and its associated inflections is translated as "religion" in Acts chapter twenty-six, verse five, and "religious" and "religion" in James chapter one, verse twenty-six and twenty-seven. With that said, the "religion of angels" is very broad in scope; however, in this book, my intent is show the "religion of angels" that Satan and his angels have been propagating since the early days of the gospel of Christ relating to some of the following: race based gospel, nationalistic based gospel, cultural based gospel, tribalism (competitive) based gospel), hedonism based gospel, and religious education based on doctrines of demons, sexual perversion based gospel, man-centered gospel, and dogmatic doctrines of men mingled with teaching of angels who do not stand in the Truth.

Satan Scheming as an Angel of Light

2 Corinthians 11:2-5, NASB: [2]*For I am jealous for you with a godly jealousy; for I betrothed you to one husband, so that to Christ I might present you as a pure virgin.* [3]*But I am afraid that,* **as the serpent** *deceived Eve by his craftiness, your minds will be led astray from the simplicity and purity of devotion to Christ.* [4]*For if one comes and* **preaches another Jesus** *whom we have not preached, or you* **receive a different spirit** *which you have not received, or* **a different gospel** *which you have not accepted, you bear this beautifully.* [5]*For I consider myself not in the least inferior to the most eminent apostles.*

Most read the verses above and do not see the religion of angels in it because maybe the Lord had not revealed it to them. However, in the verses above and some consequent verses, I will show how the prevalence of the religion of angels were then and how it is now; and as the Apostle Paul addressed this religion, so the Spirit of the Lord Jesus is also addressing it now through his holy apostles and prophets worldwide.

First, Paul equated the "serpent" who deceived the mind of Eve to some preachers who came to Corinth after Paul and were preaching "'another-similar' Jesus;" offering "'another-different' spirit," and asking the saints to "'welcome' another-different gospel." Thus, there is no doubt this "serpent" is the same serpent who is called "the 'original' serpent, the great dragon, Satan, and the Devil in Revelation chapter twelve, verse nine. It follows that this "serpent," is also called by Paul, "Satan," who is transformed into "an angel of light." And Paul called the serpent, a pseudo angel of light, Satan in context of false apostles of Satan propagating the religion of Satan. Here are the scriptures again with additional verses. It will now become a little clearer concerning the serpent's religion.

2 Corinthians 11:2-4; 13-15, NASB: *²For I am jealous for you with a godly jealousy; for I betrothed you to one husband, so that to Christ I might present you as a pure virgin. ³But I am afraid that, **as the serpent** deceived Eve by his craftiness, your minds will be led astray from the simplicity and purity of devotion to Christ. ⁴**For if one comes and preaches another Jesus** whom we have not preached, or you **receive a different spirit** which you have not received, or a **different gospel** …. ¹³**For such men are false apostles**, deceitful workers, **disguising** themselves as apostles of Christ. ¹⁴No wonder, **for even Satan disguises himself as an angel of light**. ¹⁵Therefore it is not surprising if **his servants** also **disguise themselves** as servants of righteousness, whose end will be according to their deeds.*

There you have it! Paul had established the Church of Corinth with his own pain and labor through the grace of the Holy Spirit. After which, some false apostles came through town and preached another Jesus (race based Jesus), offered a different spirit (serpent spirit), and offered a different gospel (man-centered gospel). These men Paul called "false apostles" and "servants of Satan." Hence, their messaging was from the angel, Satan, who "transformed himself into an angel of light," and therefore making the false apostles messaging a religion of the angel, Satan. If this is understood, let us now look at what Paul called the beguiling of their minds by the doctrines of the serpent, the angel Satan.

Another Jesus According to the Flesh

2 Corinthians 11:3-4, NASB: *[3]But I am afraid that,* **as the serpent** *deceived Eve … your minds will be led astray from … devotion to Christ.* *[4]For if one comes and* **preaches another Jesus** *whom we have not preached ….*

2 Corinthians 5:16-17, NASB: *[16]Therefore* **from now on we recognize no one according to the flesh;** *even though we have* **known Christ according to the flesh, yet now we know Him in this way no longer.** *[17]Therefore if anyone is in Christ,* **he is a new creature;** *the old things passed away; behold, new things have come.*

2 Corinthians 11:18-22, NASB: *[18]***Since many boast according to the flesh***, I will boast also.* *[19]For you, being so wise, tolerate the foolish gladly.* *[20]For you tolerate it if anyone enslaves you, anyone devours you, anyone takes advantage of you, anyone exalts himself, anyone hits you in the face.* *[21]To my shame I must say that we have been weak by comparison. But in whatever respect anyone else is bold – I speak in foolishness – I am just as bold myself.* *[22]Are they* **Hebrews***? So am I. Are they* **Israelites***? So am I. Are they descendants of* **Abraham***? So am I.*

The religion of angels, the religion of Satan, through Satan's false apostles, and false ministers have established a false narrative related to Jesus' "fleshly" heritage. At the Church of Corinth, false apostles came through and were exalting fleshly heritage and culture instead of the gospel of Truth, which is a "new man" (a born again believer) created by Christ, not based on fleshly heritage. Hence Paul's admonishment in second Corinthians chapter five, verses sixteen and seventeen: "Therefore from now on **we recognize no one according to the flesh;** even though **we have known Christ according to the flesh, yet now we know Him in this way no longer**. Therefore, if anyone is in Christ, he is a **new creature;** the **old things passed away;** behold, new things have come." However, the ministers of Satan propagated the superiority of race and culture of one group over another then and also now in this age.

Another Jesus Based on Culture

*2 Corinthians 11:3-4, NASB: ³But I am afraid that, **as the serpent deceived Eve ... your minds will be led astray from ... devotion to Christ.** ⁴For if one comes and **preaches another Jesus** whom we have not preached ....*

*2 Corinthians 11:18-22a, NASB: ¹⁸**Since many boast according to the flesh,** I will boast also ....²¹To my shame I must say that we have been weak by comparison. But in whatever respect anyone else is bold – I speak in foolishness – I am just as bold myself. ²²Are they **Hebrews?** So am I .....*

In second Corinthians chapter eleven, the false apostles of Satan happened to be Jews, but the same principle applies now for any race who exalt fleshy pride over Jesus' gospel of Truth. The false apostles of Satan were bosting in their "Hebrew" culture belittling the Corinthians ethnic origin. That is, they preached **"another-similar Jesus"** which had no application with regards to the new creation man anymore. Was Jesus a Hebrew? Yes! God used the Hebrew culture to bring Jesus into the world. But once that fleshly accomplishment served its purpose after Jesus' death, burial and resurrection, natural cultures were superseded by the culture of God, his unprejudiced love. Second Corinthians chapter five verses sixteen and seventeen states that "therefore from now on **we recognize no one according to the flesh;** even though **we have known Christ according to the flesh, yet now we know Him in this way no longer**. Therefore if anyone is in Christ, he is a **new creature;** the **old things passed away;** behold, new things have come." Thus, the false apostles preaching of "culture" in the days of Apostle Paul are propagating "another Jesus" seen in their boasting of being a "Hebrew." This type of gospel is the serpent's doctrine; and there are many today who have similar serpent's doctrine of division with Church practices based on Black culture, White culture, East Indian culture, West Indies culture, Judaism, as Apostle Paul said; nationality based religion, etcetera.

Another Jesus Based on Nationalism

2 Corinthians 11:3-4, NASB: *[3]But I am afraid that, **as the serpent deceived Eve** ... your minds will be led astray from ... devotion to Christ. [4]For if one comes and **preaches another Jesus** whom we have not preached ....*

2 Corinthians 11:18-22b, NASB: *[18]**Since many boast according to the flesh,** I will boast also .... [21]To my shame I must say that we have been weak by comparison. But in whatever respect anyone else is bold — I speak in foolishness — I am just as bold myself. [22]Are they Hebrews? So am I. Are they **Israelites?** So am I ....*

In addition, the false apostles of Satan were preaching a "nationalistic" based Jesus. They claimed to be superior because they were "Israelites," after the flesh, directly connected to Jesus' Israeli roots. A variation of this exists today, where many have a nationalist view of Christianity. They feel they are superior due to their race, and position on the world stage. It is worthy to note that as a result, other nations or ethnics see nationalistic based gospel as a threat and consider Christianity as race based religion and colonialism based, rather than based on the gospel of Truth (Galatians 2:11-21). **According to the Apostle Paul, the whole idea of the "gospel of Christ" for believers to become "servants to all" that we may "save some," and not the opposite of all becoming like a particular nation or culture (1 Corinthians 9:19; 22-23)!** The true Jew and the true Israelites are believers in Christ and should not be looked at from a fleshly perspective. **Note: this does not mean that a natural Jew or Israeli is not a Jew or an Israelite. On the contrary, that is their race and nationality by natural birth! However, it should not be conflated with the Truth of the gospel as Apostle Paul made it clear to Apostle Peter in Galatians chapter two.**

Galatians 2:11-14, NASB: [11]*But when* **Cephas** *came to Antioch, I opposed him to his face, because he stood condemned.* [12]*For prior to the coming of some men from James, he used to eat with the Gentiles; but when they came, he began to withdraw and separate himself, fearing those from the circumcision.* [13]*The rest of the Jews joined him in hypocrisy, with the result that even Barnabas was carried away by their hypocrisy.* [14]*But when I saw that they were not straightforward about* **the truth of the gospel, I said to Cephas in the presence of all,** *"If you, being a Jew, live like the Gentiles and not like the Jews,* **how is it that you compel the Gentiles to live like Jews?**

With that said, no believer from one nation is superior to another believer of another race. God has made believers in Jesus Christ, Jew, Gentiles, male, female, slaves, free "one" in Christ (Galatians 3:27-28). The "Jesus" we are assigned to preach is not to be nationalistic based. Yet, it does not mean that people should not love their nation, not love their heritage; however, it should not become a basis for race related competitiveness and exclusion in the Body of Christ.

Romans 2:28-29, NASB: ²⁸*For he is **not a Jew** who is one outwardly, nor is circumcision that which is outward **in the flesh.*** ²⁹*But **he is a Jew who is one inwardly;** and **circumcision is that which is of the heart, by the Spirit,** not by the letter; and his praise is not from men, but from God.*

Romans 9:6-8, NASB: ⁶*But it is not as though the word of God has failed. **For they are not all Israel who are descended from Israel;*** ⁷*nor are they all children because they are Abraham's descendants, but: "THROUGH ISAAC YOUR DESCENDANTS WILL BE NAMED."* ⁸*That is, it is **not the children of the flesh** who are children of God, but **the children of the promise** are regarded as descendants.*

Another Jesus Based on Genealogy

2 Corinthians 11:3-4, NASB: ³*But I am afraid that, **as the serpent deceived Eve** ... your minds will be led astray from ... devotion to Christ.* ⁴*For if one comes and **preaches another Jesus** whom we have not preached ....*

1 Timothy 1:3-4, NASB: ³*As I urged you upon my departure for Macedonia, remain on at Ephesus, in order that you may instruct certain men not to teach strange doctrines,* ⁴*nor to pay attention to myths and **endless genealogies, which give rise to mere speculation** rather than furthering **the administration (lit., house-law) of God which is by faith.***

2 Corinthians 11:18-22, NASB: ¹⁸***Since many boast according to the flesh,** I will boast also ....* ²¹*To my shame I must say that we have been weak by comparison. But in whatever respect anyone else is bold – I speak in foolishness – I am just as bold myself.* ²²*Are they Hebrews? So am I. Are they Israelites? So am I. Are they descendants of **Abraham**? So am I.*

The "other-Jesus" they preached was a Jesus based on genealogy. The false apostles, who happened to be Jews at that time, taught that they were superior believers because they came from the same Abraham as Jesus, according to flesh. However, Abraham is the father of us all, by faith in the "Seed," Jesus Christ (Romans 4:11-16). And "nor are they children because they are Abraham's children."

Jesus also made it clear in John chapter eight verses thirty-one through forty-nine that a person who is born in the natural lineage of Abraham can be fathered by Satan; and thus they are of their father, the Devil, even though they are of the lineage of Abraham. The same is true of Satan's false apostles Paul encountered. They are ministers of Satan, even though they claim Abraham in their lineage. This is true today when natural lineages are emphasized in Christianity above other natural lineages that may not be as prosperous or accomplished as the other (1 Timothy 1:4). When will the Church of our Lord Jesus stop preaching superiority in gene and preach the gospel of truth, "all are Christ." Again, remember that culture based religion, nationalist based religion, gene based religion, is the religion of angels, the religion of the serpent, Satan.

Another Jesus Based on Tribalism

*2 Corinthians 11:3-4, NASB: [3]But I am afraid that, **as the serpent deceived Eve** ... your minds will be led astray from ... devotion to Christ. [4]For if one comes and **preaches another Jesus** whom we have not preached ....*

*Philippians 3:2-7, NASB: [3]for we are the true circumcision, **who worship in the Spirit of God and glory in Christ Jesus** and **put no confidence in the flesh,** [4]although I myself might have confidence even in the **flesh.** If anyone else has a mind to put confidence in the flesh, I far more: [5]**circumcised** the eighth day, of the **nation of Israel,** of **the tribe of Benjamin,** a **Hebrew of Hebrews; as to the Law, a Pharisee.***

The other area of the angel Satan propagating false religion, is religion based on tribalism, we call it denominationalism or competitiveness, boasting related to religious education, etcetera. Paul in the verses above again listed boasting in nationalism, being of the "nation of Israel," as "fleshly." He also listed fleshy "culturalism," he being an "Hebrew of Hebrew" as also fleshly. Also, in this listing he added "tribalism," competitiveness, denominationalism, as fleshly; and he also listed religious education (he being educated as a Pharisees under Dr. Gamaliel), and some religious zeal as fleshly. With these thing in mind, let us read the verses again,

*Philippians 3:2-7, NASB: ²Beware of the dogs, beware of the evil workers, beware of the false circumcision; ³for we are the true circumcision, **who worship in the Spirit of God and glory in Christ Jesus** and **put no confidence in the flesh**, ⁴although I myself might have confidence even in the **flesh**. If anyone else has a mind to put confidence in the flesh, I far more: ⁵circumcised the eighth day, of the **nation of Israel**, of **the tribe of Benjamin**, a **Hebrew of Hebrews; as to the Law, a Pharisee;** ⁶as to zeal, a persecutor of the church; as to the righteousness which is in the Law, found blameless. ⁷But whatever things were gain to me, those things I have counted as loss for the sake of Christ. ⁸More than that, **I count all things to be loss** in view of the surpassing value of knowing Christ Jesus my Lord, for whom I have suffered the loss of all things and **count them but rubbish** so **that I may gain Christ**.*

The Apostle Paul said he counts these things lost so that he may gain Christ (Philippians 3:8). His education, though used by God, was "rubbish" in comparison to the knowing of Christ and experiencing the power of Jesus' resurrection. Paul **"count all things loss"** that are based on culture, race, nationalism, fleshy circumcision (exterior circumcised appearance, yet the heart is far from the living God, the "reproach of the gospel being ceased," etc.), tribalism (denominationalism, racism, etc.), institutionalized pharisaical religious hate against true believers of Jesus Christ, and so on. And the truth still holds that Paul taught, people who preach this type of "another-Jesus" are preaching a gospel of Satan; and it is the religion of angels.

False Standard of Righteousness

*Philippians 3:2-9: 2Beware of the dogs, beware of the evil workers, beware of the false circumcision; 3for we are the true circumcision, who worship in the Spirit of God and take pride in Christ Jesus, and put no confidence in the flesh, 4although I myself could boast as having confidence even in the flesh. If anyone else thinks he is confident in the flesh, I have more reason: 5circumcised the eighth day, of the nation of Israel, of the tribe of Benjamin, a Hebrew of Hebrews; as to the Law, a Pharisee; 6as to zeal, a persecutor of the church; as to the righteousness which is in the Law, found blameless. 7But whatever things were gain to me, these things I have counted as loss because of Christ. 8More than that, I count all things to be loss [c]in view of the surpassing value of knowing Christ Jesus my Lord, for whom I have suffered the loss of all things, and count them mere rubbish, so that I may gain Christ, 9and may be found in Him, **not having a righteousness of my own** derived from the Law, **but that which is through faith in Christ, the righteousness which comes from God on the basis of faith.***

*2 Corinthians 11:13-15, NASB: 13For such men are false apostles, deceitful workers, disguising themselves as apostles of Christ. 14No wonder, for even Satan disguises himself as an angel of light. 15Therefore it is not surprising if his servants **also disguise themselves as servants of righteousness**, whose end will be according to their deeds.*

The religion of angels, as manifested through Satan's false apostles, establishes their own standards of righteousness, standards that Paul rejects as "legalistic" in Philippians chapter three, and a "disguise" form of "righteousness." In Philippians chapter three, second Corinthians chapter eleven and second Corinthians chapter twelve, we learn that the false standards of righteousness offered through Satan's false apostles and/or Satan's false servants are related to how "much" gain one possessed, how "much" people and how "many" things they were "over," righteousness falsely based on having a better genealogy, better culture, superior intelligence, wearing or certain clothes, etcetera, which standards of righteousness are false. Our righteousness is acquired by faith through God's grace (Genesis 15:6, Romans 1:17, Romans 3:22, Romans 4, Philippians 3:9, Ephesians 2:8, etc.).

1 Timothy 1:3-7, NASB: *³Just as I urged you upon my departure for Macedonia, to remain on at Ephesus so that you would instruct certain people not to teach strange doctrines, **⁴nor to pay attention to myths and endless genealogies, which give rise to useless speculation rather than advance the plan of God, which is by faith,** so I urge you now. ⁵But the goal of our instruction is love from a pure heart, from a good conscience, and from a sincere faith. ⁶Some people have strayed from these things and have turned aside to fruitless discussion, ⁷wanting to be teachers of the Law, even though they do not understand either what they are saying or the matters about which they make confident assertions.*

1 Corinthians 1:26-31: *²⁶For consider your calling, brothers and sisters, that there were not many wise according to the flesh, not many mighty, not many noble; ²⁷but God has chosen the foolish things of the world to shame the wise, and God has chosen the weak things of the world to shame the things which are strong, ²⁸and the insignificant things of the world and the despised God has chosen, the things that are not, so that He may nullify the things that are, ²⁹so that **no human** may boast before God. ³⁰But it is **due to Him** that you are in Christ Jesus, who became to us wisdom from God, **and righteousness** and sanctification, and redemption, ³¹so that, just as it is written: "LET THE ONE WHO BOASTS, BOAST IN THE LORD."*

With regards to additional readings about Satan and his servants' false standards of righteousness see all of the Book of Galatians, especially Galatians chapter four; see Colossians chapter two; see Jesus's rebuke of religious standards of righteousness in Matthew chapter twenty-three, etcetera.

A Different Spirit

2 Corinthians 11:2-4; 13-15, NASB: *²For I am jealous for you with a godly jealousy; for I betrothed you to one husband, so that to Christ I might present you as a pure virgin. ³But I am afraid that, **as the serpent** deceived Eve by his craftiness, your minds will be led astray from the simplicity and purity of devotion to Christ. ⁴**For** if one comes and **preaches another Jesus** whom we have not preached, or you **receive a different spirit** which you have not received, or **a different gospel** .... ¹³**For such men are false apostles**, deceitful workers, **disguising** themselves as apostles of Christ. ¹⁴**No wonder, for even Satan disguises himself as an angel of light.** ¹⁵Therefore it is not surprising if **his servants** also **disguise themselves** as servants of righteousness, whose end will be according to their deeds.*

The other facet of the religion of angels that should be understood is that a person can receive **"'different' spirit,"** a serpent spirit, related to Satan's "covetousness" or taking advantage of the Corinthians financially, as we will see in a moment. Paul in continuing his discourse about the religion of the serpent, made it clear that those who listened to Satan's false apostles can potentially exchange the Holy Spirit already received for "another spirit."

2 Corinthians 11:3-4, NASB: *³But I am afraid that, **as the serpent** deceived Eve by his craftiness, your minds will be led astray from the simplicity and purity of devotion to Christ. ⁴**For** if one comes and preaches another Jesus whom we have not preached, or you **receive a different spirit** which you have not received ....*

2 Corinthians 12:17-18, NASB: *¹⁷Certainly I have not **taken advantage** of you through any of those whom I have sent to you, have I? ¹⁸I urged Titus to go, and I sent the brother with him. Titus did not **take any advantage** of you, did he? Did we not conduct ourselves in **the same spirit** and walk in the same steps?*

2 Corinthians 2:10-11, NASB: ¹⁰*But one whom you forgive anything, I forgive also; for indeed what I have forgiven, if I have forgiven anything, I did it for your sakes in the presence of Christ,* ¹¹*so that no **advantage would be taken** of us by Satan, for we are not ignorant of his **schemes** (lit., thoughts)..*

In second Corinthians chapter two, verse eleven, we see that Satan can get an advantage through "thoughts," Greek, "noema." "Noema" is the Greek word for "thoughts" with "ma" as a suffix. The suffix "ma" at the end of a Greek word points to the result of the action. Hence, the "result" of Satan's "thoughts" is "covetousness" or to take advantage.

That is, the Greek word translated as "take advantage" is also translated as "covetous" or "covetousness" in the scriptures. The literal definition of this Greek compound word for covetous is "pleíon," "more" and "exō," "to have." The word properly translates as "(the desire) to have more," to want a larger part, etcetera.

Hence, one of Satan's sinful thoughts is always to lust for more than allotted, or he tends to take more than allotted. It follows that Satan's religion is a religion related to greed. In addition, the Apostle Paul made it clear that a "spirit" is associated with covetous based religion. This spirit of Satan in his servants is greedy and takes advantage of others in any form.

Therefore, those who preach a false gospel that gain is linked to godliness and also covet to have more than God allotted, they have "another spirit" (1 Timothy 6:5-10). Those who believe that gain is the measure of superiority in God also have another spirit; and this spirit is serpentine or reptilian. However, as the Apostle Paul noted, he, Titus and "the Brother" walk in the "same Spirit" of the Holy God. They did not walk in "another spirit" which takes advantage of the saints of the living God.

A Different Gospel

2 Corinthians 11:2-4; 13-15, NASB: *²For I am jealous for you with a godly jealousy; for I betrothed you to one husband, so that to Christ I might present you as a pure virgin. ³But I am afraid that,* **as the serpent** *deceived Eve by his craftiness, your minds will be led astray from the simplicity and purity of devotion to Christ.* **⁴For** *if one comes and preaches another Jesus whom we have not preached, or you receive a different spirit which you have not received, or* **a different gospel** *…..* **¹³For such men are false apostles,** *deceitful workers,* **disguising** *themselves as apostles of Christ.* **¹⁴No wonder, for even Satan disguises himself as an angel of light.** **¹⁵Therefore** *it is not surprising if* **his servants** *also* **disguise themselves** *as servants of righteousness, whose end will be according to their deeds.*

Galatians 1:6-8, NASB: *⁶I am amazed that you are so quickly deserting Him who called you by the grace of Christ, for* **a different gospel;** *⁷which is really not another; only there are some who are disturbing you and want to distort the gospel of Christ.* *⁸But even if we,* **or an angel from heaven,** *should preach to you a gospel contrary to what we have preached to you, he is to be accursed!*

Paul warned the Galatian Church not to be perverted by the spurious gospel of angels that was similar to the false gospel being preached to the Corinthians Church. He warned them of "different gospel" that was being preached by men, the religion of men, and by angels, the religion of angels. What is this different gospel? This different gospel is a gospel that is man-centered rather than Jesus Christ centered. It is a gospel where men preach themselves instead of Jesus, the Christ. It is a gospel that strive to please men, especially for political favor, and so forth.

Galatians 1:10-12, NASB: *¹⁰For am I now seeking the favor of* **men,** *or of God? Or am I striving to please* **men***? If I were still trying to please men, I would not be a bond-servant of Christ.* *¹¹For I would have you know, brethren, that* **the gospel which was preached by** *me is not according to man.* ¹²*For I neither received it from man, nor was I taught it, but I received it through a revelation of Jesus Christ.*

Paul made it clear that he did not preach a "different gospel" which is a gospel according to men. Man-centered gospel is all about themselves, their riches, their popularity, and their fleshly heritage, and so forth. Paul made it clear in second Corinthians chapter four, verse five, "For **we do not preach ourselves** but Christ Jesus as Lord, and ourselves as your bond-servants for Jesus' sake." Most of what we see on television, video software, social media, etcetera are false apostles, false prophets and prophetesses, false teachers, preaching themselves. There is little mention of Jesus, if at all.

Their message for an hour or so is about raising money, their book sales, their video sales, how many following they have, they boast about being over much and tout themselves as being superior due to their abundance of money, people, and how many important people they know. They have fallen under the beguiling of the serpent and reptilian spirits and preach the man-centered gospel instead of the gospel of truth. Galatian chapter one verse ten reads as such in the Greek: **"Presently, because of men I am persuaded, or God" Or do I seem to please men. If yet I am pleasing men, I would not be a servant of Christ."** This is clear, we believe because of God. We strive to please God and not men with the gospel of Christ.

Satan's Angels Disguising as Lights

Colossians 2:18-19: *[18]Take care that no one keeps defrauding you of your prize by delighting in humility and the* **'religion' of the angels,** *taking his stand on visions he has seen, inflated without cause by his fleshly mind,* *[19]and* **not holding firmly to the head** *....*

2 Corinthians 11:2-4; 13-15, NASB: *[3]But I am afraid that,* **as the serpent** *deceived Eve ... your minds will be led astray ....* *[4]For if one comes and* **preaches another Jesus** *... or you* **receive a different spirit** *..., or* **a different gospel** *....* *[13]For such men are* **false apostles,** *deceitful workers,* **disguising** *themselves as apostles of Christ.* *[14]No wonder, for even* **Satan disguises himself as an angel of light.** *[15]Therefore it is not surprising if* **his servants** *also* **disguise themselves** *as* **servants of righteousness,** *whose end will be according to their deeds.*

There are several types of "religions" that the bible cites. "Pure religion" relates to visiting orphans, visiting widows (not just visiting them physically but also visiting by ministering the Spirit of Truth who heals the orphan spirit in humans[12]) and remaining unspotted from the world (James 1:26-27). There is "religion of the Pharisees" related to formal religious education, they also tell their followers what to do, yet they themselves don't lift a finger to do the same; and they execute dogmatic enforcement of legalism according to "their" interpretation (Acts 26:5, Matthew 23). There is "will-religion" that relates to abuse of the body with no value against the fillings of the flesh nature (Colossians 2:23). Then there is also "religion of angels," demon based doctrines mixed with men's doctrines using redemptive laws that have been made obsolete as the base of this religion.

---

[12] Jesus' solution for people who are orphans is the infilling and comfort of the Holy Spirit of Truth (John 14:16-18).

In Colossians chapter two, verse eighteen, Paul warned against the use of "religion of angels" which consist of dogmatic legalistic rules, <u>in lieu</u> of "pure religion, which includes, but is not limited to genuinely birthed believer who are **"holding firmly to the Head,"** Jesus Christ our Lord. In Paul's second letter to the Corinthians, we also hear Paul declaring that **"Satan disguises himself as an angel of light."** It follows therefore that the religion of angels may be difficult to discern because it looks like "light;" it looks like "righteousness;" because Paul equated Satan's "light" to "servants of righteousness." That is, they claim to be serving righteousness, but their righteousness is **"their own"** and not the righteousness of God by faith. In the context of Colossians chapter two, verses eighteen and nineteen , Paul was also referring to the legalistic application of redemptive laws which was now changed through Jesus Christ. However before, I speak to religious dogmatism, let me briefly show examples between God's redemptive laws that change and God's creative laws that God never changes.

Creative Laws Never Changes

In Matthew chapter nineteen, the Pharisees asked Jesus if it was okay to divorce a wife "for any cause?" Jesus' responded citing the beginning of creation and God's creative laws. The creative law says marriage is between a male and female, and that marriage joins male and female "into first flesh," oneness. This law of God that male marries female is a creative law and never changes. In addition, the creative law of "oneness" in marriage also never changes. The Pharisees then cited Moses' law allowing divorce as justification for them divorcing their wives "for any cause." Jesus, then responded not by changing God's law, but rather Jesus tells them why Moses allowed the law of divorce, in the first place. Jesus said Moses allowed divorce because of the "hardness of men's hearts." Yes, most divorce is because man or humanity have hardened their hearts against their wives. Thus, Jesus did not change God's creative law. The creative law says marriage is between male and female, only; and "what God has put together in marriage, let no man put asunder."[13]

Matthew 19:3-10, NASB: [3]Some **Pharisees** *came to Jesus, testing Him and asking, "Is it lawful for a man to divorce his wife* **for any reason** *at all?" [4]And He answered and said, "Have you not read that He who* **created** *them from the beginning MADE THEM* **MALE AND FEMALE,** *[5]and said, 'FOR THIS REASON A MAN SHALL LEAVE HIS FATHER AND MOTHER AND BE JOINED TO HIS WIFE, AND THE TWO SHALL BECOME* **ONE FLESH'?** *[6]"So they are no longer two, but one flesh.* **What therefore God has joined together, let no man separate."** *[7]They said to Him, "Why then did Moses command to GIVE HER A CERTIFICATE OF DIVORCE AND SEND her AWAY?" [8]He said to them, "Because of* **your hardness of heart** *Moses permitted you to divorce your wives;* **but from the beginning it has not been this way.** *[9]"And I say to you, whoever divorces his wife, except for immorality, and marries another woman commits adultery." [10]The disciples said to Him, "If the relationship of the man with his wife is like this, it is better not to marry."*

Redemptive Laws Change

In Hebrew chapter ten, we learn that animal sacrifices could not take away sins. These annual animal sacrifices could not make the conscious mature pertaining **not** remembering sins. The law also caused the worshippers to remember their sins every year in those yearly sacrifices. Thus, it was always God's intention to remove the temporary redemptive laws and replace them permanently with Jesus' offering for sins. The redemptive laws were only a "shadow of good things to come and **not the very 'image.'**" In fact, God never desired

---

[13] Note: Apostle Paul in first Corinthians chapter seven indicate that if divorce does occur under conditions prior to the acknowledging of the Truth, then remarrying is acceptable and not a sin. However, he encourages marrying other believers in the Lord Jesus

animal sacrifices. In Jesus' redemptive work, Jesus is the "image of the invisible God;" and once sins are forgiven, God does not remember our sins or lawlessness.

*Hebrews 10:1-10: 1For **the Law**, since it has only a **shadow of the good things to come** and not the very form of things, can never, by the same sacrifices which they offer continually year by year, make **perfect (lit., mature)** those who draw near. 2Otherwise, would they not have ceased to be offered, because the worshipers, having once been cleansed, would **no longer have had consciousness of sins?** 3But in those sacrifices **there is a reminder of sins year by year.** 4For it is impossible for the blood of bulls and goats to take away sins. 5Therefore, when He comes into the world, He says, "SACRIFICE AND OFFERING YOU HAVE NOT DESIRED, BUT A BODY YOU HAVE PREPARED FOR ME; 6IN WHOLE BURNT OFFERINGS AND sacrifices FOR SIN YOU HAVE TAKEN NO PLEASURE. 7"THEN I SAID, 'BEHOLD, I HAVE COME (IN THE SCROLL OF THE BOOK IT IS WRITTEN OF ME) TO DO YOUR WILL, O GOD.'" 8After saying above, "SACRIFICES AND OFFERINGS AND WHOLE BURNT OFFERINGS AND sacrifices FOR SIN YOU HAVE NOT DESIRED, NOR HAVE YOU TAKEN PLEASURE in them" (which are offered according to the Law), 9then He said, "BEHOLD, I HAVE COME TO DO YOUR WILL." **He takes away the first in order to establish the second.** 10By this will we have been sanctified through the offering of the body of Jesus Christ **once for all.***

God changed redemptive laws by "taking away the first" way of sacrifices for sin, "in order to establish the second," and **Jesus sacrifices for sins are the only** sacrifices we need to receive God's forgiveness. "By this will we have been sanctified through the offering of the body of Jesus Christ **once for all.** 16"THIS IS THE COVENANT THAT I WILL MAKE WITH THEM AFTER THOSE DAYS, SAYS THE LORD: I WILL PUT MY LAWS UPON THEIR HEART, AND ON THEIR MIND I WILL WRITE THEM," He then says, 17"AND THEIR SINS AND THEIR LAWLESS DEEDS I WILL

REMEMBER NO MORE." [18]**Now where there is forgiveness of these things, there is no longer any offering for sin"** (Hebrews 10:16-18).

"For when the priesthood is changed, of necessity there takes place a **change of law also**" (Hebrews 7:12).Yes, through the **changed** redemptive law, once we appropriate Jesus' sacrifice, God does **NOT REMEMBER** our sins and lawlessness going forward; and if a person feels they have to still make redemptive sacrifices to God, they are only remembering their sins in that process, and remember, animal sacrifices now have no value to a person's conscience.

Doctrines of Demons and Men

Colossians 2:18, NASB: Take care that no one keeps defrauding you of your prize by delighting in humility and the **'religion' of the angels,** *taking his stand on visions he has seen, inflated without cause by his fleshly mind ....* [20]*If you have died with Christ to the elementary principles of the world, why, as if you were living in the world, do you submit yourself to* **decrees (or, dogmatism),** *such as,* [21]*"Do not handle, do not taste, do not touch!"* [22]*(which all refer to things destined to perish with use) — in accordance with the commandments and* **teachings of men?**

1 Timothy 4:1, NASB: But the Spirit explicitly says that in later times some will fall away from the faith, paying attention to deceitful spirits and **doctrines of demons,** [3]**men who forbid marriage and advocate abstaining from foods** *which God has created to be gratefully shared in by those who believe and know the truth.* [4]*For everything created by God is good, and nothing is to be rejected if it is received with gratitude;* [5]*for it is sanctified by means of the word of God and prayer.*

The religion of angels also intermingles with the doctrines of men, whether through the religion of Pharisees or "will-religion." Paul declared that "in the latter times" (and some two thousand years later we are "in the latter times") the "doctrines of demons" would be prevalent. In addition, in Colossians, the Apostle Paul also spoke of something similar which he calls "religion of angels." The religion of angels is the conflation of "teachings of demons" and the "teachings of men" with unrealistic dogmatic rules.

Hence, Paul's warning in Colossians chapter two, verses twenty through twenty-two: "If you have died with Christ to the elementary principles of the world, why, as if you were living in the world, do you submit yourself to **decrees (or, dogmatism),** such as, **"Do not handle, do not taste, do not touch!"** (which all refer to things destined to perish with use) — in accordance with the commandments and **teachings of men?**

Demonic Teaching to Abstain from Meats

That is, the religion of angels transformed into the dogmatic teachings of men. In this case the false teaching says, you must only eat a certain kind of meat or on certain days you cannot eat meats or certain meats. As Paul said, the "doctrines of demons, men who forbid marriage and advocate abstaining from foods;" and Paul also said, "therefore no one is to act as your judge in regard to food ..." (Colossians 2:16 and 1 Timothy 4:2-3).

Demonic Teaching to Abstain from Wine

Religion of angels and teaching of demons also teach that we are not to drink wine. But Paul said, **"therefore no one is to act as your judge** in regard to food or **drink"** (Colossians 2:16). Drinking is not a sin; drunkenness is a sin. And to prove that drinking is not a sin the communion wine used in the beginning was fermented wine, so much so that over drinking of communion wine makes an abuser drunk (1 Corinthians 11:20-22). Paul also made it clear that if one wants to drink, do it in your home, at a wedding, etcetera (1 Corinthians 11:20-22, Matthew 11:19, John 2).

Demonic Teaching to Observe Certain Days

Religion of angels teach that a person must observe certain holy days (or festivals), Sabbaths, some believe that Church **must** recognize a particular saints day, pastors anniversary, Church anniversary, choir day, yearly evangelist meetings, some dogmatically teach that meetings must be held on Sundays, only, or Saturdays only, and so on. But Paul said, "therefore **no one is to act as your judge** in regard to food or drink or in respect to a **festival** or a new moon or a **Sabbath day** (Colossians 2:16). In addition Paul also said, "One person regards one day above another, another regards every day alike. Each person must be fully convinced in his own mind. He who observes the day, observes it for the Lord, and he who eats, does so for the Lord, for he gives thanks to God; and he who eats not, for the Lord he does not eat, and gives thanks to God" (Romans 14:5-6).

Demonic Teaching Forbids Marrying

Any religion that forbids marrying , is a religion instated by angels. Now before I continue, I want to make it clear that if an individual decides on their own not to marry that is acceptable. However, no individual should impose abstaining from marriage on other people. The same is true for food, drinks, etcetera. If a person decides to not drink certain drinks or eat certain food, that is fine; however, that individual should not make their belief a doctrine for the entirety of a congregation. With that said concerning the doctrine of demons that forbids marrying, it should be understood that it covers many vantage points related to marriage. This is understood in the word "forbid," which means to "estop" or prevent a person from asserting the opposite to a previous assertion.

That is, the doctrine of demons concerning marriage, encourages not getting married, if that was a person's previous assertion. The doctrines of demons encourage not to stay married if the person's previous assertion is belief in divorce. The doctrines of demons institutes marriages that do not take the form of a traditional marriage as seen today. A person's previous assertion that gender or animal species does not matter as it relates to marriage, will remain in that assertion, and cannot be convinced of God's creative law of marriage between male and female only. Also, the doctrines of demons discourage new marriages by highlighting the troubles related to marriages to make it seem better not to marry, and so on.

With all that said, the Apostle Paul made it clear that because we are now also "sons of God" through the heavenly Father's purpose for us in Christ, we are no longer under the dogmatic laws, which have become "gods," worshiping of angels and men, the false religions some are enslaved to. Therefore, "⁶because **you are sons,** God has sent forth the Spirit of His Son into our hearts, crying, "Abba! Father!" ⁷Therefore you are no longer a slave, but a son; and if a son, then an heir through God. ⁸However at that time, when you did not know God, you were slaves to those which by nature are no **gods.** ⁹But now that you have come to know God, or rather to be known by God, how is it that you turn back again to the **weak and worthless elemental things**, to which you desire to be **enslaved** all over again? ¹⁰**You observe days** and **months** and **seasons** and **years**" (Galatians 4:6-10).

Mystery Babylon, and Her Demons

*Revelation 18:2, NASB: And he cried out with a mighty voice, saying, "Fallen, fallen is **Babylon** the great! She has become a **dwelling place (lit., permanent house)** of demons and a **prison (or guard)** of every unclean spirit, and a **prison (guard)** of every unclean and hateful bird.*

This "Babylon" is "mystery Babylon, the mother of prostitutes" (Revelation 17:5). Babylon can represent the apostate church who commits spiritual and literal fornication with governments and idols of the beast systems. Babylon can also represent all religions of the earth that are merchandising, and marketing entities of every item including, but is not limited to the bodies of men and the souls of men, mingled with sexual immorality, murder, sorcery, etcetera. This mystery Babylon has also become the permanent homes of "demons." This means when any person fellowship with any earthly religion, the religion of angels, the religion of men, the teachings of demons, they are directly encountering the Babylonian houses of demons. The Book of Proverbs puts it this way. The harlot's "house is the way to hell, going down to the chambers of death" (Proverbs 7:17). Proverbs 9:18 says, in the harlot's house are "the dead" and "her guests are in hell." Thus, those who worship or seek the dead for advice are part of the Babylonian system; and in Babylon are those who fellowship with demons (1 Corinthians 10:20).

Babylon has also become a "guard"[14] of unclean spirits and every unclean and hateful bird. Yes, all Babylonian daughters protect its demons. That is, if anyone attempts to bring changes in any Babylonian expression, the people associated with Babylon, will guard against that person. Let us now look at some of the manifestations of these spirits entities in Babylon. "Demon" spirits can be defined as a "dispenser," to distribute; hence, a demon is a spirit who dispenses or distributes fortunes.

It follows that Babylon is possessed with "demons" who distributed prophetic omens to its followers. That is, most false religions of the earth also have prophetic expressions (Compare Revelation 16:13-14, 1 Samuel 18:10, Jeremia 23:13). Babylon also guards "unclean spirits." They will guard and

---

[14] See Luke 2:8 where the Greek word "phulake" used in Revelation 18:2 is translated as "guard" as guarding over sheep.

133

protect all their unclean practices, whether the uncleanness of fornication, uncleanness of same sexuality, uncleanness of sorcery, uncleanness of betrayals like Judas, and so forth. The "hateful birds" in Babylon are symbolic of "riches" that are attained through "deceit" (Jeremiah 5:27). Therefore God has commanded all of his people who are in Babylon or influenced by Babylon to leave her immediately. God does not want those who are in Babylon, and yet believe in the true God, to continue to partake of Babylon's sins! God does not want the plagues that will judge Babylon to happen to his people. Revelation 18:4-5, NASB says, "**4**I heard another voice from heaven, saying, **"Come out of her, my people, so that you will not participate in her sins** and receive of her **plagues; 5**for her sins have piled up as high as heaven, and God has remembered her iniquities."

Two Women with Wings

*Zachariah 5:5-11, NASB: 5Then the angel who had been speaking with me went out and said to me, "Now raise your eyes and see what this is that is going forth." 6And I said, "What is it?" Then he said, "This is the ephah going forth." Again he said, "This is their appearance in all the land. 7And behold, a lead cover was lifted up." He continued, "And this is **a woman** sitting inside the ephah." 8Then he said, "This is **Wickedness!"** And he thrust her into the middle of the ephah and threw the lead weight on its opening. 9Then I raised my eyes and looked, and there **two women were coming out with the wind in their wings; and they had wings like the wings of the stork**, and they lifted up the ephah between the earth and the heavens. 10So I said to the angel who was speaking with me, "Where are they taking the ephah?" 11Then he said to me, "To build a **temple (lit., house)** for her in the land of **Shinar**; and when it is prepared, she will be set there on her own pedestal."*

In the text above the angel of Lord brought to the attention of the Prophet Zachariah the view of a woman sitting inside an epha. This "woman" is then described as "Wickedness." In addition, another "two women" who had "wings" were also seen by Zachariah. These two women with wings conveyed the first woman in the epha to "the land of Shinar," another name for Babylon. This vision then can represent mystery Babylon (the woman named "Wickedness" in the epha); and the two women with wings like storks (wings used for soaring) represent female spirits or to female angels with wings who are conveying the ephah.

These two female winged spirits will also be the ones building a "house" for "Wickedness" in Shinar (Babylon or mystery Babylon). Per Bible Hub Helps Word-studies, "daímōn," one of the Greek inflections used for demons in the New Testament, is "a **feminine noun** – a demon, i.e., a fallen angel;" and this inflection is used once in the Matthew chapter eight, verse thirty-one of the "demons" who possesses two men who lived among the tombs.

Per Thayer's Greek Lexicon, "daímōn" is also used by Greek authors to describe "a god, **a goddess;** an inferiority deity ...." In addition, the Hebrew word for "spirit" ("ruach," pronounced roo'-akh) is always a "feminine noun." Thus, it should not seem implausible that there are female spirits as seen in Zechariah, chapter five, verse nine: ."... **two women were coming out with the wind in their wings; and they had wings like the wings of the stork** ...."

There is no man or woman in the natural dimension who has wings. However, in the unseen dimension, cherubs, seraphs, angels, beasts, these two women cited in this section, and so on, all have wings (Daniel 7:1-6, Revelation 4:8, Ezekiel 1:5-6). Therefore, it can be understood that there are also female spirits or female angels, some with wings, related to mystery Babylon's and her religion of angels.

This particular Babylonian expression of the religion of angels is sometimes expressed in an external or pseudo character of kindness. This pseudo kindness is understood in the definition of the Hebrew word used for "stork," which also is defined as "kindness" in the scriptures. In other words, there are many religions in the world including but not limited to some Christian denominations where outward kindness and piousness is expressed in public. However, in the private lives of the people associated with these religions there is no kindness!

Manifestations of Religious Demons

While living in North Carolina, my wife and I were attending a Church. While in one of the meetings, there was a man who happened to be sitting in front of me; and the Spirit of Jesus opened my eyes to see the invisible dimension. As I watched this man who was sitting in front of me, I saw a demon under his feet. However, as the musician of the Church began to play religious songs, I saw the demon ascend from under his feet, up to the man's knees (the man popped up out of his chair) and then the demon ascended to the man's neck and eventually to his throat, then through his mouth, and the man began to move and speak in what I call a very "religious" form that is practiced frequently in some denominations.

My wife and I visited a couple of Churches in Connecticut and Massachusetts. While attending one of the Churches, the Spirit of the Lord opened my eyes to see the invisible and my ears to hear in the Spirit. I saw a monkey-like demon jump on the back of one young man and I saw another monkey-like demon across the room jump on the shoulder of another young man. I heard these two men speak in what appeared to be "tongues of angels," not God's gifts of tongues that "speaks mysteries" to God and not the "tongues of men" (1 Corinthians 13:1; 1 Corinthians 14:2). In the Spirit, I heard one demon saying to the other "go ahead, go ahead;" except they were speaking in false tongues of angels, yet I could understand what the demons were saying in English. One demon kept inciting the other to "go ahead, go ahead." Not too long after I heard the words and saw the demons, I saw one of the men whom the monkey-demon was inciting, begin running up and down the aisle in a religious manner and a sexually effeminate manner. Most of the Church then followed this man with other falsely incite religious acts.

I observed this situation and received instruction. There are false "religions" developed by man and energized by demons that the book of Colossians calls "'religion' of angels." Note: The gift of speaking in tongues is **one of the gifts** of the Holy Spirit that confirms that a believer is filled with the Holy Spirit and sealed by the Holy Spirit. (Acts 1, Acts 2, Acts 10, 1 Corinthians 14, Ephesians 1:13, Acts 19:1-6, Acts 8, and so forth). Yet, there is a religious system called mystery Babylon that also "sits" on "tongues" and will manifest her impure religion of angels through the demons who inhabit "peoples, multitudes, nations and tongues" who she sits on, according to Revelation chapter seventeen, verses one and verse fifteen and Revelation chapter verse two (Revelation 17:1; 17:15; Revelation 18:2).

Angels are Ministering Spirits

*Hebrews 1:7: And of the angels he saith, Who **makes his angels spirits,** and his ministers a flame of fire.*

*Hebrews 1:13-14: [13]But to which of **the angels** said he at any time, Sit on my right hand, until I make your enemies your footstool? [14]Are they not **all** ministering spirits, sent forth **to minister** for them who shall be heirs of salvation?*

God, the heavenly Father, has made his "angels spirits." Therefore, any spirit, except for the Holy Spirit (who is the Spirit of God, who is the Spirit of the Lord Jesus); and except for the spirit of a human, can be considered as angels. They are considered as "angels" in light of one of the Hebrew definitions for angels meaning one who is deputized to serve God's interests; and "angels" in the sense of one of the Greek definitions as "delegates" who represent God and his interests. The archangel Michael is a spirit. The archangel Gabriel is a spirit. The angel Palmoni is a spirit. The angel Palai is a spirit. The angel Peniel is a spirit. The prince "archsoldier" in Joshua chapter five is a spirit. The prince of Persia is a spirit. The prince of Greece is also a spirit, etcetera.

In Isaiah chapter thirty-seven, verse seven , when the king of Assyria blasphemed God and Israel, the Lord said, "Behold, I will put **a spirit in him** so that he will hear a rumor and **return to his own land**. And I will make him fall by the sword in his own land." Complimentary, in Isaiah chapter thirty-seven, verse thirty-six, we learn that it was **"the angel** of the Lord" who smote one hundred eighty-five thousand (185,000) Assyrians in the night leaving "dead corps;" and "**so** Sennacherib king of Assyria … **returned** … to Nineveh." It follows that one can conclude that the "spirit" the Lord referenced in verse seven is the "angel of the Lord" in verse thirty-seven. With that said, "angels" are indeed "all ministering spirits" ("public-workers" for God) including but not limited to the original serpent and his angels, the holy angels, the elect angels, and so on. We previously learned, albeit briefly, that Satan and his angels, whom God will judge through the curse of the eternal fire, have overreached against God's plan for him to assist mankind as God originally created them to be "helpers," beginning in the garden in Eden. The writer of the Book of Hebrews makes it very clear "all ministering spirit," therefore, "all" angels are "sent forth to "minister" (lit., serve) through those who shall be heirs of salvation" (Hebrews 1:13-14). If this is understood, let us now review a few scriptural writings where angels from among God "myriads of angels" minister to God's people. We will briefly look at our Lord Jesus and the angels who ministered to him; Jacob and the army of angels with him, Elijah and the angel ministering to him, and a few personal experiences.

Angels Ministered to Jesus

Mark 1:12-13: ¹²*And immediately the Spirit drives him into the wilderness.* ¹³*And he was there in the wilderness forty days, tempted of Satan; and was with the wild beasts; and the **angels ministered unto him**.*

"Angels ministered to" Jesus after forty days of fasting. "Ministered" is one of the two words translated as "minister" in the Book of Hebrews chapter one, verse fourteen relative to angels serving God's heirs. The first word translated as "minister" in Hebrews chapter one, verse fourteen is defined as "people worker, public worker, etcetera. The second word translated as "minister," means to serve, to run and errand kicking up dust in the process, and deacon. In Mark chapter one, verse thirty-one, "when the angels "ministered to Jesus, they "ran errands" for him. They served him; and since he was hungry after forty days of fasting, they probably fed him "angels' food" (Psalms 78:25).

In addition, like Gabriel who strengthened Daniel after twenty-one days fasting, the angels who ministered to Jesus also strengthened him after forty days of fasting. Jesus was also among the wild beasts in the wilderness during his fast; and I am quite sure as the angel shut the mouths of the lions when Daniel was unjustly forced to spend overnight in the den, so the angels prevented wild beasts from harming Jesus.

It is also worthy to note that extensive fasting, in Jesus's case forty days, causes an encounter with the angel named Death who kills with plagues, sword, hunger (or famine), and wild beast (Revelation 6:8). That is, "hunger" and "wild beasts" are two of the killing tools of death; and Jesus overcame both hunger and wild beast during the forty days of fasting, Jesus' angels also helping him in his humanity. Yes, even our Lord Jesus was "served" by ministering angels.

Elijah ate Angels' Food

*Psalm 78:25: Man did eat **angels' food**: he sent them meat to the full.*

*1 Kings 19:5-7: [5]And as he lay and slept under a juniper tree, behold, then **an angel** touched him, and said unto him, **arise and eat**. [6]And he looked, and behold, there was a **cake baked** on the coals, and a cruse of water at his head. And he did eat and drink …. [7]And the angel of the LORD came again the second time, and touched him, and said, **arise and eat**; because the journey is too great for you.*

In Mark chapter one, verse twelve and thirteen, the angels may have also ministered to Jesus by giving him angels' food **after** Jesus fasted forty days. In Elijah's case, the angel fed him "angel's food" and water **before** he embarked upon the forty days fast. In this case the angel ministered to Elijah "strength" before Elijah's forty days of fasting. In addition, with respect to Elijah's encounter with this angel there were other angelic activities happening against Elijah from Jezebel, which highlight even more why "an angel of the Lord" was dispatched to minister to Elijah. Elijah had just slain four hundred-fifty (450) of Jezebel's prophets of Baal. Baal being understood to be Satan according to Jesus in Matthew chapter twelve. King Ahab, Jezebel's husband, told Jezebel what Elijah had done to the prophets of Baal. She became incensed and sent "messenger" to Elijah of her intent to kill him. It follows that Elijah eventually "saw" the apparent "messenger" he ran for his life (1 Kings 19:1-3). However, this "messenger" that Elijah saw may have been angels (Satan's angels) sent by Jezebel.

Here is the logic behind this principle. Jezebel was highly developed in "witchcrafts"—whispering spells. She was a Satan worshiper, because "Baal" is "Satan," the "prince of demons"(Matthew 12:24-26). Above, I made the point that "all" angels were originally created to serve humanity including the angels who have submitted to Satan.

Thus, since Jezebel was a sorcerer, a worshiper of Satan ("Baal"), the messengers who approached Elijah were possibly an angel of darkness that Jezebel sent. The practice of using serpent spirits is also seen with the diviner Balaam's attempt to curse Israel through serpents' enchantments in Numbers chapters twenty-two through twenty-four. And be reminded that any who practice such things with the angels of darkness can expect God's judgment if they don't repent (Exodus 22:18, 1 Chronicle 10:13).

Jocob and the Army Angels

Genesis 32:1-6: [1]*And Jacob went on his way, and **the angels of God** met him.* [2]*And when Jacob saw them, he said, this is God's host: and he called the name of that place Mahanaim.*[15] [3]*And Jacob sent 'angels' before him to Esau his brother unto the land of Seir, the country of Edom.* [4]*And **he commanded them,** saying, thus shall ye speak unto my lord Esau; your servant Jacob saith thus, I have*

---

[15] Two Camps

sojourned with Laban, and stayed there until now: ⁵And I have oxen, and asses, flocks, and menservants, and women-servants: and I have sent to tell my lord, that I may find grace in your sight. ⁶And the 'angels' returned to Jacob, saying, we came to your brother Esau, and also he comes to meet you, and four hundred men with him.

Jacob encountered the angels of God when he was experiencing what is known as "Jacob trouble" relative to meeting his brother Esau, he previously tricked out of his birthright. During Jacob's preparation for the encounter with Esau, which he thought would be potentially bloody and for obvious reasons, he prayed to his God, the God of Abraham and Isaac, the God of our Lord Jesus Christ. God responded to Jacob by sending an army of angels. This tells us that Jacob had a good cause to be worried because the situation was obviously edgy and potentially explosive in order for God to send an army of angels. And God did eventually diffuse the encounter into a peaceful encounter once Jacob acknowledged that he was indeed a trickster. Upon Jacob's acknowledgment of his old nature, God changed his name and nature to Israel. With that said, allow me to show you some principles concerning angels with regards to Jacob and the ministering angels.

As one reads Genesis chapter thirty-two, verses one through six and also Genesis chapter thirty-two, verses twenty-eight through thirty-two, it is clear that angelic activities are present. There is an army of the angels of God. Jacob eventually wrestled with a "God angel" who I believe is called Peniel. However, there is another reference to angels that is overlooked. In Genesis chapter thirty-two, verse three and verse six, "Jacob sent **'angels'** before him to Esau his brother" and "he commanded them" what to do and "the **'angels'** returned to Jacob" with an assessment of the situation. The Hebrew writings of Genesis chapter thirty-two, verses three through six did not say that Jacob sent before him "servants" as it says in Genesis chapter thirty-two, verse sixteen. Instead, it says he sent "angels" and the "angels returned to him." This is a true understanding[16] since the topic of the entire chapter of Genesis chapter thirty-two is about "the angels of God" who came to be "ministering" spirits to Jacob; and Jacob saw these angels (Genesis 32:1). In this case, the angels also served him "working-publicly," as one of the definitions for ministering means as cited in Hebrews chapter one, verse fourteen.

Thus Jacob sent angels to Esau and commanded them what to say; and they went and made an assessment and returned to Jacob. However, these angels did their ministering publicly for Jacob with regards to Esau. Here is what the angels reported to Jacob in Genesis chapter thirty-two, verse six. "We (the angels) came to your brother Esau, and also he comes to **meet** you ...." Their report was telling; because the word "meet" means to encounter accidently, friendly, or violently." Hence, the angels assessed that the potential was there for a violent conflict.

God, seeing this potential for violence beforehand, sent the angels of God to assist Jacob. Jacob, then using his authority as an "heir of salvation" sent angels before him to Esau to appeal to his brother and to assess the spiritual climate. In addition, after Jacob saw the gravity of the situation towards him and his young family, he had no way out but to finally face his nature as the angel wrestled with him that night to get Jacob to acknowledge his trickster nature, which he did. And the living God was able to turn away Esau's wrath through Jacob's wiliness to change. **Because when Esau met him, Esau did not meet "Jacob," he met the prince "Israel" whom God had changed by the blessing of the angel!**

---

[16] Note: Even though this author believes the "messengers" Jacob sent to Esau could very well be "angels ... sent forth to minister 'through' them who shall be heirs of salvation" (Hebrews 1:13-14), everyone must be persuaded in his or her own mind with respect to this opinion.

Angelic Experiences

Jesus and His Army of Angels

May 6, 1996: I (Judith) was asleep and was attacked by an evil spirit. I fought off and drove away this evil spirit by rebuking it. I saw and heard myself saying this in my sleep, "Jesus has overcome you" and the dark spirit left, and immediately I saw another vision. In this vision, I saw Jesus on a white horse with a sword, He ran toward this other army full of horsemen. I noticed Jesus was alone, but the other army had a lot of men. As they raced towards one another and fought, I heard the angels singing very loudly, and it was sounding in my ears. The song of the angels declared, **"He has overcome them, He has overcome them, He has overcome them ..."** As this part of the dream or vision finished, God took me upward and I ascended in the air and through the clouds. As I ascended, I heard another song of angels singing loudly, **"For He is worthy, for He is worthy."** This song was also sounding in my ears. I saw heaven and New Jerusalem. It was beautiful. The temple was gold, and the streets were gold. The color of heaven was the color of the rainbow, beautiful. As I looked, it finally dawned on me that I was in heaven. I thought to myself, "this is where we will be; and it had to be where Jesus is." As the vision continued, I felt like I was flying; and I thought to myself, "I see why Jesus was able to go through walls and move from point to point in a split second after his resurrection." I continued upward and went through some more clouds. It seemed like I came to an end. At this end, there was a mist or cloud. I knew God the Father or Jesus had to be behind this cloud. I thought to myself, "I will finally get to lay at Jesus' feet and see Him in person." After these things, I awoke so elated I woke my husband and told him about the vision.

An Angel and Two Skull-like Hills

Around March 1993, in a vision from the Lord Jesus, I (Donald) saw two hills that were shaped like skulls. An angel then took a hold of me and whisk me between the two (2) skulls like a speeding whirling wind. (I understood these two skull-like hills to mean the witness (2) of being crucified in sufferings. Jesus was crucified in a place called Skull, Hebrew Golgotha.) I was then transported by/with the angel again as he walked with me around the trailer we were living in at the time, and he measured around the trailer with a measuring reed that he had in his hand. He then testified to me that in six months I would be moving from the trailer. We eventually moved from Jacksonville, North Carolina to Baltimore, Maryland after additional prompting from the Holy Spirit.

Supernatural Mechanic

The summer of 1987, my first car, a 1982 Ford Escort, needed the brakes and rear lights to be fixed before I (Donald) would be granted permission to use my vehicle on base (I was a Marine stationed at Camp Jejune, NC). At the time, I did not have enough money to fix the car; thus, Judy and I prayed to the Father. I specifically asked him to fix the car brakes and car lights for us. Shortly thereafter (it was the next day) we realized that the Lord Jesus sent an angel to fix both brakes and the lights supernaturally, without human's hands. This was apparently done by a ministering angel. In Deuteronomy chapter eight, verse four God says, "your 'clothe did not fail' upon you, neither did foot swell, these forty years." Thus, I know, the heavenly Father also repaired my car by the hand of his angel(s).

Stranger Angels

*Hebrews 13:2: Do not neglect to show hospitality to **strangers,** for by this some have entertained **angels** without knowing it.*

Angels sometimes appear as strangers. In Judges 13, the angel that appeared to the father and mother of Sampson were not familiar with the visitor and thought he was a man of God at first. They showed hospitality and later learned he was an angel of the Lord sent with blessings for both of them. In Genesis chapter eighteen, "three men" appeared to Abraham and Abraham was courteous by receiving them and feeding them. It was later understood that one of the men was the Lord Jesus, himself and the other two were angels with the Lord. In Genesis chapter nineteen, we learned that Lot received the same two angels that were with the Lord when Abraham met them, and Lot received them into his house and also fed them. Thus, it is common for angels to appear as humans and strangers; and we are to respond to strangers with hospitality.

Angels as Young Men

*John 20:11-13, NASB: [11]But **Mary** was standing outside the tomb, weeping; so as she wept, she stooped to look into the tomb; [12]and **she saw two angels** in white **sitting, one at the head and one at the feet, where the body of Jesus had been lying.** [13]And they said to her, "Woman, why are you weeping?" She said to them, "Because they have taken away my Lord, and I do not know where they put Him."*

*Mark 16:1-6, NASB: [1]When the Sabbath was over, **Mary** Magdalene, Mary the mother of James, and Salome bought spices so that they might come and anoint Him. [2]And very early on the first day of the week, they came to the tomb when the sun had risen. [3]They were saying to one another, "Who will roll away the stone from the entrance of the tomb for us?" [4]And looking up, they noticed that the stone had been rolled away; for it was extremely large. [5]And* entering the tomb, **they saw a young man sitting at the right,** wearing a white robe; and they were amazed. ⁶But he said to them, "Do not be amazed; you are looking for Jesus the Nazarene, who has been crucified. He has risen; He is not here; see, here is the place where they laid Him.

Luke 24:1-5, NASB: ¹But on the first day of the week, at early dawn, they came to the tomb bringing the spices which they had prepared. ²And they found the stone rolled away from the tomb, ³but when they entered, they did not find the body of the Lord Jesus. ⁴While they were perplexed about this, behold, **two men suddenly stood near them in gleaming clothing;** ⁵and as the women were terrified and bowed their faces to the ground, the men said to them, "Why are you seeking the living One among the dead?

Mary encountered "two angels" on the day of Jesus' resurrection according to John as cited above. They appeared in the form of the two cherubs at both ends of the Ark of the Covenant, Moses made. In addition, Mark described one of these angels as a "young man" in white robe. Luke described them as "two men" in gleaming clothes. Thus, angels can appear as men and young men. Angels appear as strangers, a person not familiar to the locals of a community. They appear as young men. They appear as men. Yet, in their appearance as men, they sometimes are clothed in white robes or gleaming clothes. Having said that, I will give a couple of experiences I had with strangers whom I have later determined were angels.

Strange Strong Looking Man

Around the summer of 1990, I was in great distress as I processed whether or not I should move from Baltimore, Maryland back to North Carolina. One day while doing drywall work on a renovation for a Church in Baltimore City, I went out back (for what I cannot remember). As I was out back, a strange strong looking man walked past me. I never saw the man before, and never saw him afterwards. He was a stranger to me. As he walked by, he looked at me very sternly and said, decide what you want to do. As he spoke, he did not stop, but kept walking. He was an angel sent from the Lord Jesus in the form of a stranger. I knew then that the choice was mine whether to move to North Carolina or not and the Lord expected me to decide. I did decide to move to North Carolina, as the Lord was calling me. In addition, when we finally packed up to move, I saw and heard in a vision that I was like Elisha who crossed the Jordan to receive the double portion of the mantle of His spiritual father (Elijah); and that I would return to Baltimore to do the work of the Lord Jesus; and so it is.

Ugly Looking Stranger

Another encounter with a stranger happened to me, at a time in my life when I was struggling with my own self-esteem. After I got out of the United States Marine Corps, I experienced extreme poverty that eventually caused such grief in me to the point of rejecting myself. However, God used this impoverished situation to help heal my mind. In my mind, I was treating people the way I felt about myself. I realized that the bad feeling I had towards myself, is the way I may have been previously treating the poor. Therefore, God used the situation to heal me. Thus, I can now help someone else. With this in mind, the event took place in my first year in Engineering School.

One day, while waiting for a Math class to begin, a strange looking young man came to me asking for directions to a copier. The stranger was so disfigured in the face that it was difficult for me to look at him. I was so "stunned" at his disfigurement, to the point that I didn't even want to talk to him or be seen with him (compare Jesus' disfigurement and lack of beauty cited in Isaiah chapter fifty-two, verse fourteen and Isaiah chapter fifty-three, verse two).[17] Because of these inner feelings, I began to cry within, holding back the tears without. The emotions I was feeling while talking with the young man was related to an understanding of the Lord's ugliness that was unveiled to me the night before, as part of the heavenly Father's process of healing me internally.

I felt, in my heart, that I had denied the Lord Jesus. Again, the reason this denial was so disturbing to me was the Lord had taught me about Jesus' ugliness the night before I met this strange man. The Lord instructed me the night before of His ugliness to comfort me in my ugliness (my ugly situation that eventually deeply affected my self-esteem). Thus, in my initial rejection of the stranger, I fulfilled the Scripture in Isaiah chapter fifty-three, verse three; because in essence, I rejected Jesus' ugliness also. "And we hid as it were our faces from Him...." Yes, all of "we" (us) have denied the Lord's ugliness (Isaiah 53:2).

Yes! All of "we" are sometimes still ashamed of Him. If anyone does not believe that we all denied Him (His ugliness), take a look at the pictures of Jesus those men and women have on their walls. Some have Him portrayed as a handsome Black man, or a good-looking white man. These pictures deny the true look of Jesus' ugliness.

Nonetheless, I did embrace the stranger's disfigurement, and I helped him; after I heard those words, again, resound in me ("And we hid as it were our faces from Him"); and these words I heard in the moment of the encounter with the stranger also straightened my internal struggles. I did eventually get myself together and helped the young man find the room he was looking for.

---

[17] You may refer to my book, *The Ugliest Man God Made*

In helping him, I embraced the Lord's ugliness myself. But the idea that I had denied the Lord's ugliness exemplified in this stranger was painful. Afterwards, I concluded that the stranger was an angel sent by God. He entered the rooms he asked me to help him find; and he did not exit the room; and I never saw him again on campus or off campus. He was apparently a stranger the Lord deliberately sent to test me; and to heal me. As said in Hebrews chapter thirteen, verse two, "be not forgetful to entertain strangers; for thereby some have entertained angels unawares."

Human Angels

*Revelation 8:2: And I saw the **seven angels** who stand before God, and to them were given seven trumpets.*

*Revelation 1:20: The mystery of **the seven stars** which you saw in My right hand, and the seven golden lampstands: **The seven stars are the angels of the seven churches**, and the seven lampstands which you saw are the seven churches.*

There are indeed seven angels that stand before God. These seven angels can be considered literal archangels or other angels. In the Talmud, only four archangels are listed: Michael, Gabriel, Raphael, and Uriel; and according to "1 Enoch," portion of which Jude quoted in the Book of Jude, there are Michael, Gabriel, Raphael, Uriel, Raguel, Saraqâêl, and Remiel. Nevertheless, please note that every person has to be persuaded in their own minds with regards to the archangels listed above. Yet the angels in the Book of Revelation, including but not limited to the apparent two sets of seven angels, have applications to the Lord Jesus and Jesus' human angels of his Churches.

Seven Angels of the Churches

*Revelation 1:20: The mystery of **the seven stars** which you saw in My right hand ... **the seven stars are the angels of the seven churches** ....*

The Lord himself said that the "stars" in his right hand were "angels of the seven Churches." These angels are the overseers of the Church. One must also realize that the words spoken by the Lord in Revelation chapter two through Revelation chapter three were spoken directly to the "angel of [that] Church." These seven angels are also symbols of all the messengers of the Church of Jesus Christ. That is, each one of these seven messengers or "seven angels" are representative of apostles, prophets, teachers, evangelists, pastors, and elders. However, I know the question will be asked, how can a single angel represent apostles, prophets, evangelists, pastors, and teachers? In Revelation chapter seven, verses two and three, we learn that the "angel" (singular)" is really **many** angels, also called **"we."** The scriptures said, "I saw **another angel (singular)** ascending from the east, having the seal of the living God. And **he (singular)** cried with a loud voice … 'Do not harm … till **we (plural)** have sealed the servants of our God on their foreheads.'" As one can see, the **"we"** are in reality the **"another angel"** and the **"he."** Thus, this singular angel is considered a plurality of angels.

Human Angels of Churches

Also, remember I stated above that our Lord Jesus did not address the Church members themselves until towards the end of each of His discourse. In Jesus' discourse to the respective "angel of the Church," Jesus' language tells the reader that the "angels" are representative of human beings. The angel of the Church of Smyrna is asked to be "faithful unto death"(Revelation 2:10). Angels do not die natural deaths (Luke 20:36). Angel can only die through the Second Death, the Lake of Fire (Revelation 20:14, Revelation 20:11, Matthew 25:41). Thus, the angels of the Churches are humans. With that said, let us also look at another example relative to the angel of the Church of Thyatira to show that the angel of this Church was married; and therefore, a human angel.

Revelation 2:18-20; 22, NASB: [18]*"And to the angel of the church in Thyatira write: The Son of God, who has eyes like a flame of fire, and His feet are like burnished bronze, says this:* [19]*'I know your deeds, and your love and faith and service and perseverance, and that your deeds of late are greater than at first.* [20]*'But I have this against you, that you tolerate* **the woman (or the wife of-you**[18]**)** *Jezebel, who calls herself a prophetess, and she teaches and leads My bond-*

---

[18] This translation is per ISA 3 Interlinear Analyzer of the Byzantine Texts.

*servants astray so that they commit acts of immorality and eat things sacrificed to idols. ²¹'I gave her time to repent, and she does not want to repent of her immorality …. ²²'Behold, I will throw her on a bed of sickness, and those who **commit adultery with her** into great tribulation, unless they repent of her deeds.*

As one reads all the words that were spoken to the angel of the Church of Thyatira, we can see that **this angel was married**. "The **woman**¹⁹ Jezebel" is Jezabel is **"the wife"** of the angel of the Church or she is **"your wife"** – the wife of the angel of the Church. Angels in heaven are not permitted to marry (Luke 20:35-36). But the human angels of the earth can marry. Also, Jezebel in the Old Testament was married to king Ahab, a leader of "Israel" called "the **Church** in the wilderness" in Acts, chapter seven, whose wife Jezebel dominated him.

The Jezebel, in Revelation chapter two, is also married to the leader of the Church, because the text clearly says in Revelation chapter two, verse twenty-two that she "committed adultery," an act that can only be done by a married person. Finally, as Ahab was reluctant to stop Jezebel's practices of witchcraft, idolatry, the angel of this Church also was allowing his wife to do unacceptable practices. Hence, Jesus' admonishment to the angel of the Church to repent, change his mind, about allowing Jezebel to teach inappropriate doctrines.

Prophet Angel

*Revelation 22:8-9: ⁸Now I, John, saw and heard these things. And when I heard and saw, I fell down to **worship before the feet of the angel** who showed me these things. ⁹ Then he said to me, "See that you do not do that. **For I am your fellow servant, and of***

---

¹⁹ The Greek word "guné" is translated as both woman and wife.

your brethren the prophets, *and of those who keep the words of this book. Worship God."*

In the verses above, we see John, the beloved apostle, wanted to worship the angel that showed him some events that occurred after the seven angels poured out their bowls of wrath. In fact, it was one of the angels who poured out the bowls of wrath that John tried to worship (Revelation 21:9). John said, **"I fell down to worship before the feet of the angel who showed me these things."** However, the angel had a surprise for John. First: the angel would not allow "angel worship." Instead, the angel said, **"Worship God!"** Second: the angel said he was **"of the prophets."**

Yes, the angels that poured out the bowls of wrath are "prophets" (humans); they are also called "slaves" of the Lord; and they are also called "of those who keep the words of this book." Thus, we see that some of the angels in the Book of Revelations are also called "prophets."

Ascending and Descending Angels

In John chapter one verse fifty-one, Jesus also referenced angels who appear to be men of God. The activities of the angels that Jesus referenced in John chapter one verse fifty-one appears to be humans who originated their activities from the earth seen in the fact that they "ascended" first, before they "descended."

*John 1:51: And He said to him, "Most assuredly, I say to you, hereafter you shall see heaven open, and the **angels of God ascending and descending** upon the Son of Man."*

*Genesis 28:12: Then [Jacob] dreamed, and behold, a **ladder** was set up on the **earth,** and its top reached to heaven; and there the angels of God were **ascending and descending** on it.*

The angels described by Jesus did **not** start their journey in heaven, same as the ones that Jacob saw at the ladder in

154

Genesis chapter twenty-eight, verse twelve. Jesus did **not** say these angels would be first descending and then ascending. On the contrary, these "angels of God" would be "ascending" from the earth, as Jacob saw them ascending from the earth, to hear a message from the Lord God and then "descending" back to the earth to disburse their message. Remember that Paul, an apostle also called himself an "angel of God;" and Paul ascended and descended between third heaven and earth (2 Corinthians 12:1-4). The apostle John also migrated between heaven and earth (Revelation 4:1-2) Jesus himself said that He was on earth and in heaven at the same time (John 3:13, KJV).

Paul, "as an Angel of God"

As I indicated earlier in this book, **John the Baptist,** whom Jesus credited as the greatest prophet to live, was called a **"messenger (lit., angel)"** in Malachi chapter three, verse one and Matthew chapter eleven, verse ten. Our Lord Jesus is also called "the Messenger," the Angel, in Malachi chapter three, verse one. Therefore, it is not strange that apostles and prophets are also called angels. Again, Paul, an apostle also likened himself to an "angel of God."

*Galatians 4:14: And my trial which was in my flesh you did not despise or reject, but you received me as an **angel of God**, even as Christ Jesus.*

Two things can be taken from the verse above that is full of spiritual understanding. Paul said the Church of Galatia received him as Christ Jesus. This should not be strange; since the Body of believers who have been baptized into Christ in the Holy Spirit **"is** Christ." "For as the body is one and has many members, but all the members of that one body, being many, are one body, **so also is 'the' Christ.** For by one **Spirit,** we were all baptized into one body" (1 Corinthians 12:12-13). "For **all of you** who were **baptized into Christ** have **clothed** yourselves with **Christ"** (Galatians 3:27). Paul also said the believers a Colosse "have put on the new self who is being renewed to a true knowledge according to the image of the One who created him—a renewal in which there is no distinction between Greek and Jew, circumcised and uncircumcised, barbarian, Scythian, slave and freeman, **but Christ is all, and in all**" (Colossians 3:10-11).

The same is true concerning Paul being received as an "angel of God." Jesus, His holy Apostles, and prophets, for sure, are also called angels; and apostles and prophets are among the angels in the Book of Revelation who release the judgments of God in the waters, earth, air, etc. "Be glad over her, O heaven, and ye holy apostles and prophets, because God did judge **your judgment** of her" (Revelation 18:20, YLT)! This being said, Jesus may have also called His apostles angels in Luke chapter nine, verse fifty-two through fifty-four to "internally prepare" the people to receive him. As previously stated, the Bible called the prophet, John the Baptist an "angel;" and the Bible says priests are also called "angels" (Malachi 2:7). The prophet Malachi called John, the Baptist an angel. Malachi also called Jesus "the Angel." The Prophet Haggai is also called an angel (Haggai 1:13).

Jesus and John as Angels

*Malachi 3:1: "Behold, I send **My messenger (lit., My angel)**, and he will prepare the way before Me. And the Lord, whom you seek, will suddenly come to His temple, even the **Messenger (lit., Angel)of the covenant**, in whom you delight. Behold, He is coming," Says the LORD of hosts.*

*Luke 7:26-28: [26]But what went ye out to see? a prophet? Yea, I say unto you, and much more than a prophet. [27]This is he of whom it is written, Behold, I send **my messenger (lit., my angel)** before your face, who shall prepare your way before thee. [28] I say unto you, among them that are born of women there is none greater than **John**: yet he that is but little in the kingdom of God is greater than he.*

156

It is clear from the references that "my messenger" is John, the Baptist, as also witnessed by the Lord Jesus Himself. In addition, "the Messenger of the Covenant" is Jesus, whom Malachi called "the Lord." "And **the Lord** who you seek ... even **the Messenger** of the covenant." Jesus is the Lord of the eternal Covenant. Jesus is also "the Angel who suddenly came to His temple."

With all that said, it appears to me that the seven angels with the seven trumpets are "prophetic apostles," (apostles who are prophetic) and "apostolic prophets." (prophets with apostolic revelation). Paul said, "You received me as an **angel of God**" (Galatians 4:14). John "saw the **seven angels** who stand before **God** and to them were given seven **trumpets**" Revelation 8:2). Trumpets are equated to prophets who sound the prophetic word of the Lord to encourage his people, warn his people or utter judgments (Ezekiel 33:1-7).

"The angel ... said ... I am your fellow **servant,** and of your brethren **the prophets**" (Revelation 22:8-9). Thus, the seven angels include but are not limited to apostles, prophets, prophetic apostles, and apostolic prophets (these are foundation ministries of the Church of which Jesus, the chief foundation Stone). The foundation of ministry (singular) of apostles and prophets are authorized to release predictive words, judgments or justice, and directive words (Ephesians 2:20, Ephesians 3:4-5, Acts 5, Acts 13, Acts 14, etc.).

Apostles and Prophets

Note: The five-fold ministries (apostles, prophets, teachers, evangelist, and pastors) can sometimes function in dual offices. That is, the legitimate sons of God functions in all the offices as the heavenly Father wills it to be. Peter was a pastoral apostle (John 21:16, 1 Peter 5:1-4). Jesus said that John, the Baptist, was an "apostolic prophet" (a prophet with apostolic overtone); because Jesus said John the Baptist was **more than** a prophet (Luke 7:26).

John, the beloved apostle was a "prophetic apostle," one of the Twelve Apostles of the Lamb who is also prophetic (Revelation 22:9). Paul was a prophetic-apostle, preacher-apostle, and a teacher-apostle (1 Timothy 2:7). The Apostle Barnabas was either a teacher and apostle or a prophet and an apostle (Acts 13:1, Acts 14:14).

Angels and their Powers

*Genesis 3:24, NASB: So He drove the man out; and at the east of the garden of Eden He stationed **the cherubim** and the **flaming sword** which turned every direction to guard the way to the tree of life.*

God's angels are gifted with various powers or weapons of power. In Genesis chapter three we see the first mention of "a flaming sword" and "cherubs." Both of these entities were sent as "guards" of the way to the tree of life. The power of the "flaming sword" is not like the swords men use. The Hebrew word for "flaming" in Genesis chapter three, verse twenty-four is used of "flaming enchantment" in Exodus chapter seven, verse eleven that was used to transform rods into "dragons."

Thus, it is possible that the "flaming sword" guards the way of the tree of life with its ability to transform the "sword's" power into another form. This is substantiated by the fact that the flaming sword "turns." The Hebrew word translated as "turn" also means to "change" and is used by king Saul whose heart was "changed" after an encounter with the Seer Samuel (1 Samuel 10:9). Also, the release of the powers of spiritual swords is executed when the sword is drawn from a sheathe. Here is an example of the angel of the Lord with his drawn sword and the power of the unsheathed sword.

Unsheathed Sword

*1 Chronicle 21:14-16, NASB: [14]So the LORD sent a **pestilence** on Israel; 70,000 men of Israel fell. [15]And God sent an angel to Jerusalem to destroy it; but as he was about to destroy it, the LORD saw and was sorry over the calamity, and said to the destroying angel, "**It is enough; now relax your hand.**" And the angel of the LORD was standing by the threshing floor of Ornan the Jebusite. [16]Then David lifted up his eyes and saw the angel of the LORD* *standing between earth and heaven, **with his drawn sword in his hand stretched out over Jerusalem.***

Satan tempted David to number the people of Israel. This was a grave sin apparently due to his motive. The Lord then sent "an angel of the Lord" to discipline David for numbering the people. In the pestilence released by the angel, seventy thousand (70,000) men of Israel died. However, a lot is revealed in the discourse of God with the angel. As the pestilence was working havoc and about to destroy Jerusalem, the Lord said to the angel "it is enough now, relax your hand." David also saw the angel with a "drawn sword in his hand stretched out over Jerusalem." This then shows that the pestilence was a result of the angel's drawn sword. That is, when the angels' sword is sheathed, no plague is released. However, the unsheathing of the sword is the release of the plague. There is power in the sword of the angel who can unsheathe it to release pestilence at the command of the Lord (see also Numbers 22).

Wings Like Hawks

*Psalm 78:25: Man did eat **angels' (abbîrîm)** food: he sent them meat to the full.*

*Psalms 78:25, Septuagint (LXX): Man ate **angels' (Greek: angelōn)** bread; he sent them provision to the full.*

We know explicitly that cherubs and seraphs have wings. Cherubs have four wings, and seraphs have six wings. We also know that the archangel Gabriel can fly according to the Book of Daniel chapter nine. As we learn previously in the chapter on "Religion of Angels," some female spirits have "wings like storks." Thus, as God highlighted what types of wings the two women spirits have; so likewise, it seems important to show some of the wing types of other angels and their power (ability) of flight.

In Psalm chapter seventy-eight, verse twenty-five, we see the use of the phrase "angels' food." The word translated as "angels" is a Hebrew word "abbîrîm" that means "mighty one that soars" or "mighty one that flies." "Abbîrîm" was translated in the Greek Septuagint (LXX) as "angels." Therefore, an understanding of the word "abbîrîm" is that of angels' specifically, of mighty angels who fly and soar. That is, the root word for "abbîrîm" and its derivatives has the meaning of "mighty one," as in, "Mighty God," strong, valiant, etcetera (Strong's #47, #82). "Abbîrîm" is derived from a primitive root meaning to soar or to fly. This meaning is exemplified in the use of the Hebrew word "abar" in the Book of Job, relative to the skill, wisdom and understanding of a hawk in flight.

*Job 39:26: Does the **hawk fly (Hebrew: abar)** by **your wisdom**, and stretch her **wings** toward the south?*

Since "angels" are considered flyers of the Mighty God, or soarers of the Mighty God, or mighty soarers, mighty flyers, what is their flight like? Their flight and their wings are like the skillful and speedy hawks. That is, the angels of the Lord are exceptionally skilled in their flight like hawks; and some have wings like hawks; and they fly with the speed of hawks. The Hebrew word for hawk means "flashing speed," to shine to glimmer.

That is, they are so fast in flight, their speed is like a flash of light! The "hawk fly by [God's] wisdom;" or literally, the "hawk fly by [God's] understanding." It is interesting to note that the Hebrew word picture, or hieroglyphics understanding of "abbyr" (אָבִּיר) is that of the head or mind [resh (ר)] of "my father" [abi (אָבִּי)]. They apparently can ascertain the mind of the heavenly Father, or the thought of the heavenly father is in them!

It follows that the "ability" (power) of the angels' flight is by God's "understanding" and "wisdom." In addition, in contrast to the "two women" with "wings like storks" related to the apostate Babylonian system, some angels have **wings like hawks**, agile in flight, speedy in flight, and skilled in maneuvers, to be able to find their intended target or landing spots!

Daniel 9:21, ESV: ... the man **Gabriel,** *...came to me in* ***swift flight*** *("muap biap") ....*

Daniel 9:21, Septuagint (LXX): ... the **man Gabriel** *...* **came flying** *("petomenos") ....*

With regards to the archangel Gabriel's flight to bring Daniel understanding from the Lord, by looking at both the Hebrew word used for his flight ("yaeph") and the Greek translation for the same word used for Gabriel's flight ("petomenos"), we understand that Gabriels mode of travel to Daniel was by "flying;" and there was some "weariness" involved in Gabriel's flight. With regards to Gabriel's weariness, it was related to warfare with the invisible prince of Babylon who attempted to resist both he and his fellow archangel, Michael from revealing to Daniel that which was noted in the writing of Truth.

Thus, we now understand through the scriptures of Truth that angels also have the power of flight. Angels have wings; and some of their wings are like the wings of hawks. Having said that, here is a brief list of the type of other angels' wings. In Daniel chapter seven, we see that some beasts in the spirit have wings.

The spirit beast that represented Babylon was a lion with "eagle's wings;" and spirit beast that represented Greece was a leopard with "four wings of a fowl" (Daniel 7:1-6). In the Revelation chapter four, we see that one of the living beings, the seraphim, was a "flying eagle" (Revelation 4:7). This flying eagle apparently has wings like the eagle (Revelation 8:13) . Therefore, it is safe to say that some angels, in addition to cherubs, seraphs, do have wings; and thus have the power of flight.

Automatic Abilities

Acts 12:6-10, NASB: *[6]On the very night when Herod was about to bring him forward, Peter was sleeping between two soldiers, bound with two chains, and guards in front of the door were watching over the prison. [7]And behold, an **angel of the Lord suddenly appeared**, and **a light shone** in the cell; and he struck Peter's side and woke him up, saying, "Get up quickly." And **his chains fell off his hands**. [8]And the angel said to him, "Gird yourself and put on your sandals." And he did so. And he said to him, "Wrap your cloak around you and follow me." [9]And he went out and continued to follow, and he did not know that what was being done by the angel was real, but thought he was seeing a vision. [10]When they had passed the first and second guard, they came to the **iron gate that leads into the city, which opened for them by itself;** and they went out and went along one street, and immediately the angel departed from him.*

Peter was imprisoned by Herod to be killed as Herod had previously imprisoned and beheaded Apostle James, the brother of the beloved Apostle John. However, this time through prayers of the saints, God sent an angel to rescue Peter. In this event some of the abilities of angels are also revealed. The angel's presence had the ability to shine light in the prison. That is, the spirit angel had the ability to shine his light in the natural dimension to give Peter light.

Also, the chains on Peter automatically fell off through the presence and ability of the angel. In addition, the angel had the power to "automatically" open the iron gate to lead Peter out of the various gates of the prison. This shows God's abilities in the angels he created. In Acts chapter twelve, verse twenty-three, we also see that angels of the Lord can just

163

"strike" a person to cause death. King Herod was struck by the angel and Herod died immediately. Thus, angels have "automatic" abilities where things are done automatically through their presence, touch, words, etcetera.

Gabriel and His Word

Luke 1:18-20, NASB: [18]*Zacharias said to the angel, "How will I know this for certain? For I am an old man, and my wife is advanced in years."* [19]*The angel answered and said to him,* **"I am Gabriel, who stands in the presence of God, and I have been sent to speak to you and to bring you this good news.** [20]*"And behold,* **you shall be silent and unable to speak** *until the day when these things take place,* **because you did not believe my words, which will be fulfilled in their proper time."**

The archangel Gabriel appeared to Zachariah, the father of John, the Baptist, to tell him that his prayer requesting to have a baby is answered. However, the unbelieving heart of Zachariah was exposed even though his prayer was answered. Do we do the same sometimes?

We pray for something and when we are told our prayers will be answered we respond in doubt. Gabriel's response to Zachariah's unbelief was not pleasant and shows the delegated authority angels of the Lord have. Gabriel, emphasized to Zachariah who he was and caused Zachariah to be unable to talk for about nine months.

Gabriel said, "I am Gabriel (mighty of God) who stands in the presence of God." But Gabriel did not stop there, Gabriel showed the power of making things happen through his word. Gabriel said to Zacharia, "you shall be silent and unable to speak until the day when these things take place, because you did not believe my words." And yes, Zachariah did not speak again until John the Baptist was born in order to give him his name of John and not Zachariah (Luke 1: 57-66). With that said, Gabriel's ability to speak things into existence through God's rhema word is consistent with his character. He spoke to Mary that God's powerful prophetic word would come to pass with regards to Jesus and his virgin birth through her. And the word he previously spoke to Zachariah about him and Elisebeth having John, the Baptist in their old age also happened as Gabriel said.

Angelic Power of Touch

Acts 12:21-23, NASB: [21]*On an appointed day Herod, having put on his royal apparel, took his seat on the rostrum, and began delivering an address to them.* [22]*The people kept crying out, "The voice of a god and not of a man!"* [23]*And immediately an angel of the Lord* **struck him** *because he did not give God the glory, and he was eaten by worms and died.*

Daniel 10:18-19, NASB: [18]*Then this one with human appearance* **touched me** *again and strengthened me.* [19]*He said, "O man of high esteem, do not be afraid. Peace be with you; take courage and be courageous!" Now as soon as he spoke to me, I received strength and said, "May my lord speak, for you have strengthened me."*

In Acts chapter twelve, verse twenty-three, the angel "knocked" Herod and he was eaten by worms and died. The demonstration of God's power in this angel is not that Herod was eaten by worms, because all humans are consumed by worms at death unless embalmed. The miracle in this angel's act was the speed by which Herod was eaten by worms and died, all from the result of touch. In Daniel chapter ten, the Prophet Daniel experienced the power of angel's touch in a positive way. In Daniel's case both the "touch" and the "words" of the angel strengthened Daniel. Thus, we see that angelic touch can be used to kill and can be used to strengthen. It is important to note at this time that Satan, the accuser of the brothers, also exercises powers. I want to highlight this to the reader so that you may not be deceived by him. In the Book of Job, after Satan set his heart on Job to test Job, the Lord allowed Satan to test Job with events. Thus, when the house fell down of Job's children that was the work of Satan. It was Satan who energized the "Sabeans" to kill Job's servants. When the fire from heaven burned Job's livestock, that fire was Satan's (see also Revelation 13:11-13). The "great 'spirit'" that caused the house to collapse on Job's children was Satan's spirit; and finally, the sickness Job experienced was Satan's smiting. Thus, we must be able to know when the angels of the Lord are working powers related to "truth," and when Satan and his angels are working powers that relate to lies or accusations. There is a difference!

Angels and the Elements

There exists some of God's "elect angels" who control, or have mastery over the wind, the sea, the waters, the times, etcetera. Again, for emphasis, they only exercise this power and authority as the Lord Jesus commands (Psalm 103:20). Let us note some of these examples in the Scripture. I will start first in the Book of Revelation.

*Revelation 7:1: And after these things I saw **four angels** standing on the four corners of the earth, holding the four **winds** of the earth, that the wind should not blow on the earth, nor on the sea, nor on any tree.*

One can see here that the **"four angels"** had the ability to control the **"wind"** that it "should not blow" on the earth. This "wind" can be interpreted as both literal wind and spiritual wind related to the "wind of doctrine" (see Ephesians 4:14). There is an **"angel of the waters."**

*Revelation 16:4-6, NASB: ⁴Then the third angel poured out his bowl into the rivers and the springs of waters; and they became blood. ⁵And I heard **the angel of the waters** saying, "Righteous are You, who are and who were, O Holy One, because You judged these things; ⁶for they poured out the blood of saints and prophets, and You have given them blood to drink.*

This angel had the authority to change to blood the waters of rivers and waters of springs through a bowl of wrath. This angel can be considered as one of the spirit angels who has control over the waters. Or this angel can be considered as one of the prophets of "the spirits of just men made mature" who are called angels and exercise authority over water as Moses and Aaron (Hebrews 12:23, Revelation 22:8-9, Exodus 7:20). John also saw "another angel came out from the altar, which had **power (lit.; authority) over fire...**"

*Revelation 14:17-20: ¹⁷And another angel came out of the temple which is in heaven, and he also had a sharp sickle. ¹⁸Then **another angel**, the one **who has power over fire**, came out from the altar; and he called with a loud voice to him who had the sharp sickle, saying, "Put in your sharp sickle and gather the clusters from the vine of the earth, because her grapes are ripe." ¹⁹So the angel swung his sickle to the earth and gathered the clusters from the vine of the earth, and threw them into the great wine press of the wrath of God. ²⁰And the wine press was trodden outside the city, and blood came out from the wine press, up to the horses' bridles, for a distance of two hundred miles.*

This angel of the altar (the Golden Altar) has authority to combine the fire of the Golden Altar with the incense (prayers) of all saints and to scatter the fire-incense into the earth as protection for God's royal priesthood. In Revelation chapter eight, verse five, the angel took the censer mixed with fire of the Golden Altar and scattered the mixture into the earth before the plagues in the Book of Revelation begin. In the Book of Leviticus, we learn that God commanded the use of incense mixed with fire to protect the High Priest from death (Leviticus 16:12-13). This principle holds in Revelation chapter eight verse five; however, the angel did not do the same in Revelation chapter fourteen. That is, this angel of the fire also has the authority **not** to release the fire mixed with incense for protection, but instead can direct the reaping of the grapes of "vines of the earth" without any protection through prayer (incense) mixed with God's fire that fumigate the prayers into God's nostril as a sweet smell. Thus, the grapes of "vines of the earth," having no protection of frankincense mixed with prayer, are to experience the winepress of the wrath of God (Revelation 14:18-20).

Angelic Blessing

Genesis 48:14-16, NASB: [14]*But* **Israel** *stretched out his right hand and laid it on the head of* **Ephraim,** *who was the younger, and his left hand on* **Manasseh's head** *...* [15] *and he* **blessed Joseph** *and said ...* [16]*The* **angel** *who has redeemed me from all evil,* **bless the lads;** *and may* **my name** *live on in them, and the* **names of my fathers Abraham and Isaac;** *and may they grow into a multitude in the midst of the earth."*

Finally, I would like to leave the reader with blessings from our Lord Jesus Christ and all the holy and elect angels of his presence. As the patriarch "Israel" invoked blessings upon the sons of Joseph through **"the angel"** who redeemed him for his trouble related to Esau, may the elect and holy angels release these blessings to you also (Genesis 48:14-16). May the name of Jesus, the Lamb of God, be named in your forehead giving you the mind of Christ (Revelation 3:12, 2 Corinthians 2:16, Revelation 14:1). May the name Israel, the "Israel of God" be named upon you (Romans 9:6-8, Galatians 6:13-16, Romans 2:28-29).

May the name of our father of faith, Abraham, and or father of the promise of Isaac be named upon you (Romans 4:16, Romans 9:6-8). May all the blessings of our God and Father of our Lord Jesus Christ who has blessed us will all spiritual blessings in the heavenlies, in Christ, be upon you! May you inherit jointly with Jesus Christ!

*Ephesians 1:3-4a: **Blessed** be the God and Father of our Lord Jesus Christ, **who has blessed** us will **all** spiritual **blessings** in heavenly places in Christ: According as he has chosen us in him before the foundation of the world ....*

The Melchizedek priesthood, or the royal priesthood or the holy priesthood, who overcome through faith in Jesus and overcome as declared in Revelation chapters two and three inherit all things through Jesus. We inherit the Holy Spirit (Galatians 3:14-18; 3:29; Ephesians 1:13-14). We inherit the kingdom of God (Matthew 25:34, James 2:5). We inherit the living hope of incorruptible salvation (1 Peter 1:4-5, Hebrews 1:14). We inherit the world with Abraham through faith in Jesus (Romans 4:13-14). We inherit glory related to resurrection bodies (Romans 8:17-23), inheriting sonship (son-placing (Galatians 4:7); inheriting eternal life (Titus 3:7); inheriting all things (Hebrews 1:2; Revelation 21:7); inheriting righteousness through faith (Hebrews 11:7); inheriting land [Matthew 5:5, also the profit of the land is for all (Ecclesiastes 5:9)]; **inheriting the name "son" [the name that is above angels** (Hebrews 1:4); husbands and wives inheriting blessings [(good words) 1 Peter 3:9]. And more importantly, God, the heavenly Father, himself, is our inheritance (Ezekiel 44:28).

Notes

Notes

Other Books

Wisdom from Above, by Judith Peart
Procreation, Understanding Sex, and Identity, by Judith Peart
100 Nevers, by Judith Peart
The Shattered and the Healing by Judith Peart
The Lamb, by Donald Peart
Jesus' Resurrection, Our Inheritance, by Donald Peart.
Sexuality, By Donald Peart
Forgiven 490 Times, by Donald Peart w/Judith Peart!
The Days of the Seventh Angel, By Donald Peart
The Torah (The Principle) of Giving, by Donald Peart
The Time Came, by Donald Peart
The Last Hour, the First Hour, the Forty-Second Generation, by Donald Peart
Vision Real, by Donald Peart
The False Prophet, Alias, Another Beast V1, by Donald Peart
"the beast," by Donald Peart
Son of Man Prophesy Against the false prophet, by Donald Peart
The Dragon's Tail, Prophets who Teach lies, by Donald Peart
The Work of Lawlessness Revealed, by Donald Peart
When the Lord Made the Tempter, by Donald Peart
Examining Doctrine, Volume 1, by Donald Peart
Exousia, Your God Given Authority, by Donald Peart
The Numbers of God, by Donald Peart
The Completions of the Ages ... by Donald Peart
The Revelation of Jesus Christ, by Donald Peart
Jude—Translation and Commentary, by Donald Peart
Obtaining the Better Resurrection, by Donald Peart
Manifestations from Our Lord Jesus ...by Donald and Judith Peart).
Obtaining the Better Resurrection, by Donald Peart
The New Testament, Dr. Donald Peart Exegesis
The Tree of Life, By Dr. Donald Peart
The Spirit and Power of John, the Baptist by Dr. Donald Peart
The Shattered and the Healing by Judith Peart
Is She Married to a Husband? by Donald Peart
The Ugliest Man God Made by Donald Peart
Does Answering the Call of God Impact Your Children? by Donald Peart

Victory Out-of-the Beast-the Harvest of the Earth by Donald Peart
The Order of Melchizedek by Donald Peart
Ezekiel-the House-the City-the Land (Interpreting the Patterns) by Donald Peart
Butter and Honey, Understanding How to Choose the Good and Refuse Evil by Donald Peart
Wholly Maturing and Wholly Inheriting, Spirit, Soul, and Body, by Donald Peart
Angels and the Supernatural, by Donald Peart

Contact Information:
Crown of Glory Ministries
P.O. Box 1041 Randallstown, MD 21133
donaldpeart7@gmail.com

Donald Peart Biography

Donald Peart is married to Judith Peart. Donald committed his life (though for a short period) while Judith recommitted her life to the Lord Jesus around the summer of 1981 after the pair kept reading the Book of John and the book of Revelation. Donald read the entire Book of Revelation and became especially interested in Revelation 20:4. Eventually, in April 1986, Donald and Judith permanently recommitted their lives to the Lord Jesus. They have been serving the Lord Jesus since and declaring the well-message of Jesus, the Christ. Over the years, the Lord Jesus has worked various manifestations of signs, wonders, and miracles through them. Below are three examples of the Lord Jesus' involvement in the lives of Donald and Judith.

In 1988, while living in North Carolina, the voice of the Lord spoke to Donald and said, "I have not called you to be an apostle, pastor, evangelist, teacher, but a ...(Donald blocked out the rest of the words the Lord was speaking to Him; because at the time, Donald was afraid God would call him to function in a ministry contrary to what Donald believed he should be functioning as--a prophet)." Approximately seventeen years later, on February 6, 2005, in Maryland, while Donald was on a fast; on the 13th day of the fast, the Lord Jesus resumed the conversation he had with Donald in 1988. As Donald listened, the voice of the Lord continued exactly as He spoke in 1988, "I have not called you to be a prophet, an apostle, an evangelist, a pastor, or teacher, but I have called you to be a son."

In 1990, while in prayer speaking to the heavenly Father about going to university to study engineering, Donald heard the Lord Jesus say to him "you are as Joseph before me; go to engineering school; you will be good at it." The Lord also said to Donald, "this is the sign that I have spoken to you; your wife is pregnant with a girl." Donald responded to the Lord saying, "Joseph did not have any daughters." To which the Lord replied, "Joseph is a fruitful son, a fruitful son by a well whose daughters run over the wall." Donald immediately searched the Scriptures to see if Joseph had any daughters. The Scriptures confirmed that what the Lord spoke to Donald was correct. Genesis 49:22, translated from the Hebrew, states "Joseph is a fruitful son, a fruitful son by a well whose daughters run over the wall." The "sign" the Lord gave to Donald was fulfilled immediately. Judith Peart was already pregnant with their third child; a girl named Charity was born to them according to the time of life. Donald also graduated from engineering school. In addition to their five natural children, they have spiritual "daughters" and "sons" because God is fulfilling His word to them. This was also the second and third time the Lord called Donald a son.

On a day around 1991, Donald became disheartened, and he spoke to the Lord about his circumstances. At the time, he and his wife were experiencing extreme trials after Donald's obedience to the Lord. Donald was instructed to study God's Word exclusively, which turned out to be almost four years of intense study and prayer coupled with a time of consistent acute trials or probe-testing. As Donald sat on the sofa that day reading Genesis 2, the Lord began unveiling to Donald an understanding of Genesis 2 with an understanding he had not heard the elders teach. The Spirit of the Lord began to show Donald the sequence of creation, including the man (Adam), the original serpent, and Mrs. Adam (later called Eve).

As the Spirit of Jesus revealed to Donald how the Scriptures in Genesis chapter two should be interpreted, his mind began questioning what he was reading and hearing in the Spirit. His mind questioned the revelation of the Holy Spirit due to previous doctrines he learned in church from the elders and commentaries. As Donald questioned the understanding the Spirit of God revealed to him, Donald saw the pages of the Bible he was reading being closed one by one, yet the physical Bible in his lap was still open to the same pages he was reading. This is when he realized he was seeing a vision. The Lord then said to him, "Do not filter My Word through what the elders have taught you."

As a result of the Lord making Himself know to Donald and Judith throughout the years and providing explicit directions to Donald with regards God's doctrine, Donald and Judith have preached the gospel of Christ as the Lord has taught him; a gospel that is centered on Jesus Christ, the Son of the living God and the bride of Christ. With that said, the Lord Jesus has also graced Donald to earn diplomas from Baltimore Polytechnic High School; an Associate of Arts degree in Pre-Engineering, a Bachelor of Science degree in Civil Engineering, a Master of Science in Construction Management, and a Doctorate in Theology.

Made in the USA
Middletown, DE
31 December 2023

46831360R00106